D1483351

SPOOK OR SPOOF?

The Structure of the
Supernatural in Russian
Romantic Tales

Delbert D. Phillips

UNIVERSITY
PRESS OF
AMERICA

Library of Congress Catalog Card Number: **81-40838**

TABLE OF CONTENTS

CHAPTER ONE

INTRODUCTION

One of man's strongest emotions is fear--apprehension of the unknown and of death. His greatest hope is that the personality may not be snuffed out at the moment of demise but that some form of transcendental reality indeed exists. It is only natural that these concerns would find their way into literary expression. At the present time we are experiencing a renaissance of belief in the supernatural. Popular literature is replete with tales of spirits, ghosts, and reincarnation. Such preoccupation with the supernatural was common also to antiquity.

During the Greek and Roman eras the fantastic often served as the basis for literary endeavor. There were, for example, Petronius' story of the werewolf and the horrific passages from Apulius. Lucian wrote of a haunted sandal, and Phlegon's On Wonderful Events contains the story of a corpse-bride. Early literature of the supernatural is manifest also in the old Icelandic Edda and the Nibelungenlied of the Teutonic world.

The supernatural is encountered also in the famous eighth-century English epic Beowolf, the Arthurian legends, ballads, and in Chaucer's Canterbury Tales. It remained for Dante to develop the technique of depicting a supernatural atmosphere in literature. The macabre is present also in Sir Thomas Malory's "Mort d'Arthur," and demonic elements are found in "Dr. Faustus" of Elizabethan drama as well as in the witch and ghost scenes of "Hamlet."[1]

The body of supernatural literature grew throughout the seventeenth and eighteenth centuries and gave rise to the birth of the Gothic school of horrific and fantastic prose. The gothicists were to exert an important influence on Russian prose of the first decades of the nineteenth century.

Typical contributions to early Gothic literature were provided by the haunted landscapes of Ossian, the visions of William Blake, the witches of Burns' "Tam O'Shanter," Coleridge's demonistic "Christabel" and "Ancient Mariner," and the spectral beauty of Hogg's "Kilmeny." German contributions were Burger's "Wild Huntsman" and the celebrated ballad of "Lenore" with its chilly demon-bridegroom. Thomas Moore adapted from Teutonic sources the legend of the ghost statue-bride in his ballad of "The Ring," and Goethe's classic masterpiece, Faust, is considered the highest achievement of Gothic literature.

It was Horace Walpole who became the founder of the supernatural tale as a permanent fictional form. In 1764 he published the "Castle of Otranto," a tale which soon became known for its treatment of the weird and ghastly. In England Mrs. Aiken responded with an unfinished fragment, "Sir Bertrand" (1773), with its trappings of terror and an animated corpse. Clara Reeve followed with "The Old English Baron" (1777), a highly acclaimed tale with a single ghostly inhabitant.

A new talent soon emerged, Mrs. Ann Radcliffe, whose novels of supernatural horror and suspense set new elevated standards in the area of the supernatural, even though the famous authoress chose to present complex natural rationalizations for the uncanny. The Mysteries of Udolpho (1794) is considered the best of her six novels which were published between 1780 and 1826. It was Radcliffe who was to prove the most influential of the English Gothicists in Russia.

Literature of the supernatural achieved even greater heights through the productivity of Matthew Gregory Lewis whose most famous work, The Monk (1796), earned its author the appellation of "Monk" Lewis. In the hands of Lewis the Gothic horror tale became even more violent and was saturated with the influence of Teutonic legends which had not been used by Radcliffe. Also known for the drama, "The Castle Spectre" (1798), for his Tales of Horror (1799), Tales of Wonder (1801) and for a number of translations, Lewis expands the Gothic line and succeeds in initiating the destruction of the Radcliffian tradition.

A final figure in the line of European Gothic writers was the Irish clergyman Charles Robert Maturin, who created the masterpiece of supernatural horror, "Melmoth, the Wanderer" (1820), in which the Gothic tale attains heretofore unscaled heights of horror. Fantastic literature fared well also in the work of E.T.A. Hoffmann (1776-1822), whose tales were probably the most influential of all on Russian literature of the supernatural. Important also was the productivity of Friedrich Heinrich Karl, whose "Undine" (1814) has been hailed as the most artistic of the supernatural tales produced on the Continent.[2]

It was during the 1820's that the supernatural tale was first manifest in Russian literature with the appearance of fantastic short stories in Russian literary journals and almanacs. Early translations of English, French, and German origin soon yielded to original Russian products. Exemplary of these early translations was "The Nocturnal Journey," an excerpt from the novel Adventures of Hugh Trevor by Thomas Holcroft.[3] Nocturnal travellers who lose their way encounter a corpse. A similar tale is "The Terrible Night in the Desert," written under the name of K. Bonafon.[4] The narrator becomes lost in a remote area on a dark night. The fantastic elements here are limited to the depiction of atmospheric conditions.

4

Probably the first native Russian production in this early horrific literature was Bestuzhev's "A Page from the Diary of a Guard Officer," dated 1821.[5] Hunters encounter a skull on a dark night, are captured by bandits and are about to be murdered when the narrative is abruptly terminated with the statement that it was all a dream. The influence of Radcliffe is felt in the remark that the hunters were out in a "Radcliffian" night. Radcliffe was to prove an important influence on Bestuzhev's creativity in the fantastic vein.

Bestuzhev further allies himself with Gothic traditions in his castle tales of terror and mystery, "Venden Castle," "Neygauzen Castle," and "Eyzen Castle," which appeared between 1823 and 1825.[6] Also in 1825 Bestuzhev proved himself adept in Gothic methods through the presentation of an atmosphere of "sweet terror" in "The Traitor," which details the story of Prince Vladimir Sitskiy of Pereyalslavl'. This tale is extremely suspenseful with generous doses of the horrific in the witchcraft scene.[7]

A typical example of the ghost story in this early period of supernatural literature is "The Dream," by F. Glinka.[8] The narrator of this tale walks in a churchyard and encounters the ghosts of those buried in the cemetery there. An animated corpse is present in "The Grave Digger,"[9] and stories of were-wolves appeared in the periodical News of Literature in 1825[10] and in the almanac Snowdrop in 1829.[11]

The Faust-Mephistopheles theme is sometimes found in these early tales. Typical is "The Old Acquaintance,"[12] in which a young poet is guided through the world by an old man who alleges to be Mephistopheles. This tale like so many others is constructed as a dream. The oriental tale is also represented in this early fantastic literature. An example is "The Magic Glass," which appeared in 1831.[13]

These tales of the 1820's and early 1830's proved to be the initial works in a genre which was to be well practiced in the creativity of the great writers of the first decades of the nineteenth century. Such early tales were usually translations or were heavily influenced by foreign models. The stories contain supernatural elements which vary from the depiction of atmospheric conditions to the actual appearance of supernatural beings. Each story is provided with rational interpretation for supernatural phenomena, usually as dreams or hallucinations.

5

Discussions of the supernatural in literature appeared in journalistic reviews, collections, and articles. Typical in this respect was N.A. Polevoy's review of Odoevskiy's Motley Fairy Tales, in which he attributes the human inclination toward belief in the supernatural to religious superstition inherent in the nature of man.[14] However, in a review of Pogorel'skiy's The Double, S.P. Shevyryov justifies the existence of the supernatural as a manifestation of a separate world governed by its own laws.[15]

The views of Sir Walter Scott on the supernatural were soon to find their way into Russian journals. Scott wrote a prefatory memoir to the novels of Ann Radcliffe which appeared in Russian translation in 1826 on the pages of the journal Son of the Fatherland.[16] Scott argues that the public of his day strictly demands an explanation for the supernatural. Ghosts and witches should be allowed, he affirms, since at one time they were universally avowed as factual. Therefore, it should not stretch the reader's credulity to require him when reading about his ancestors to believe for a short time in what they themselves affirmed to be true. Yet the actual management of the supernatural is a matter of the utmost delicacy.

Scott does not present a solution to the problem of the supernatural. He concludes that on the whole perhaps the most artistic solution of all is for the author to leave something in the dark, since the normal course of events consistently conceals so many incidents. As a result there are the means of compounding the taste of two different types of readers, those who demand an explanation for each circumstance and incident of the narrative, and those who possess more imagination and need not require that all transnormal phenomena be restored fully to commonplace reality. Indeed, Scott admits that the story writer is placed in a difficult situation and dilemma. It is expected that his story be interesting and even extraordinary. Yet he should not explain his wonders by referring them to banal causes because of the resulting triteness, nor should the story explanation be attributed to supernatural powers because of the resulting incredibility.

A translation of another of Scott's articles, "On the Supernatural in Fictitious Composition," appeared three years later also in Son of the Fatherland.[17] In this article Scott traces belief in the supernatural to man's religion as well as to the principles of his nature and mental faculties. He notes that practitioners of Christianity believe that there was a time when divine power showed itself visibly on earth. Scott suggests that belief in the supernatural will lessen as mankind becomes more enlightened, and that those who claim to have experienced the transnormal are suffering a temporary delusion.

6

According to Scott the supernatural in fiction must be managed with great delicacy since the effect is exceedingly difficult to sustain. The marvelous should be presented in small portion since it loses its effect by being continually apparent, and the imagination of the reader should be excited but not gratified at the same time. Incidents should be dark and indefinable by nature, with manifestation of the supernatural a brief, rare, and indistinct phenomenon originating from a being so different as to be totally incomprehensible. The first encounter with the otherworldly is the most effective and may be weakened or defaced by subsequent recurrence. The supernatural being should not appear too often, nor should it become loquacious or speak at all if rendered subject to human sight.

Scott also points out that when a particular style tends to become antiquated, caricatures or satirical imitations of it give rise to a new genre. He notes the presence of what is termed a comic side of the supernatural in which the writer parodies the miracles which he transmits. The reader will perceive that the old style is travestied instead of made the object of serious attention.

Articles such as Scott's, reviews, translations, and original Russian tales were the initial manifestation of a growing Russian interest in the supernatural. It was during the third decade of the nineteenth century that the supernatural tale was to receive extensive literary development in the work of such writers as Somov, Pogorel'skiy, Bestuzhev, Odoevskiy, Pushkin, Gogol', and Vel'tman.

The first significant treatment of the supernatural tale came from the pen of A. Pogorel'skiy,[18] whose "Poppy-Seed-Cake Seller of the Lafyortov District" appeared in the March 1825 edition of News of Literature. Supernatural elements in this tale include a witch's incantation, a tomcat in human form, an animated corpse, and several visits by the ghost of the old poppy-seed-cake seller herself. Mysterious events such as the ill luck which befalls those who denounce the old woman as a witch and the sudden collapse of the deceased's house add supernatural coloration to the tale.

Also of interest are the supernatural tales of O. Somov,[19] a little-known writer of the early nineteenth century. Somov provided a number of fantastic tales including "The Monster" and "A Command from the Other World."[20] "The Monster," an early example of skaz[21] in Russian literature, is narrated in the colorful peasant dialect of a coachman and is the story of a prosperous peasant family which is allegedly visited by a friendly folk-monster called "Kikimora." "A Command from the Other World" is

7

a typical parlor tale of the supernatural in which a mysterious ghostly knight appears claiming to have come from the world beyond the grave seeking a meeting with the living.

Supernatural tales which were structurally more complex were supplied by A. Bestuzhev[22] who composed three mature stories of the preternatural, "An Evening at the Caucasian Waters in 1824," "The Terrible Divination," and "The Cuirassier: A Partisan Officer's Tale."[23] "An Evening at the Caucasian Waters" is simply a series of anecdotes framed with dialogue. The supernatural is initially encountered in a dragoon captain's story of his brother who attempted to shake hands with a hanging corpse. An artillerist then recalls his uncle's confrontation with an apparition in an old abandoned manor house. Finally, a young hussar narrates his own somewhat similar experience with ghosts in a Uniat village where he had sought lodging one stormy night.

In "The Terrible Divination" Bestuzhev reaches the height of his romantic style with the climax of this tale forming one of the most horrific scenes in Russian literature. "The Cuirassier" is also anecdotal in structure, the narrative uniting two separate anecdotes framed within one main story. The brooding Zarnitskiy tells how he once explored a legendary old castle and was accosted by a ghost.

Like Bestuzhev, V.F. Odoevskiy[24] was also thoroughly interested in portraying the supernatural. From the initial stages of his literary career Odoevskiy was to experiment with the concept of combining heterogeneous tales into a general frame tale within which a group of speakers would exploit the philosophical implications of the various stories. The result of these experiments was the publication of such a grouping of tales under the heading Russian Nights. The plan for this work as well as the composition of the individual tales occurred between 1831 and 1835.

The supernatural is initially encountered within three of these tales which comprise the Fourth Night: "The Brigadier," "The Ball," and "A Corpse's Mockery." "Brigadier" and "A Corpse's Mockery" present live corpses. In "The Ball" the reader is accosted by a whole bevy of skeletons which writhe and knock their bones against one another. Another of Odoevskiy's supernatural tales in this same vein is "The Live Corpse," in which an unseen ghost is present at its own funeral. Odoevskiy's single ghost story of the traditional type is entitled "The Apparition," in which four travelers spin ghost yarns in order to pass the time.

Like Odoevskiy, A.S. Pushkin[25] also expressed an interest in the supernatural. With Pushkin the otherworldly surfaces in three prose tales. The first of these, "The Solitary Cottage on Vasilevskiy Island," contains disguised devils, supernatural forces, and a mysterious cab bearing the cabalistic number 666. In "The Undertaker" poor Adrian Prokorov is visited by the ghosts of his former "clients." Finally "The Queen of Spades" is an intriguing tale of madness with heavy doses of the supernatural.

Perhaps no Russian writer embarked upon greater flights into the supernatural than did N.V. Gogol'[26] whose stories veritably bristle with fantastic events, personages, and powers. Most important in this respect are the Ukrainian Tales which appeared in two collections and evidence the author's interest in the otherworldly. "The Fair at Sorochinsy," for example, stars the Devil who has been chased out of Hell and is rumored to be in the Sorochinsy neighborhood in search of his shirt. In "St. John's Eve" the Devil assumes human form and enters into secret trysts with the young cossack Petro. The comic element predominates in "The Lost Letter" and "A Place Bewitched" which also concerns various devilish machinations. Perhaps the most horrific of all Russian tales is "Viy" from the Mirgorod cycle. In this tale the demonic intrudes directly without motivation from the real world.

The supernatural is encountered also in three other Gogolian short stories, "The Portrait," "The Overcoat," and "The Nose." In "The Portrait" the painter Chertkov obtains a painting of an old man with uncannily lifelike eyes. The ghost of this elderly gentleman miraculously climbs down from the frame and promises the painter success if he will forsake his art for money. Gogol' was perhaps dissatisfied with this tale for he later reworked it and reduced or eliminated the fantastic elements altogether.

An apparition is present also in "The Overcoat" in which the ghost of poor Akakiy Akakievich returns to take revenge on those who had wronged him in life. A different sort of tale is "The Nose" in which Collegiate Assessor Kovalyov awakens one morning to discover that his nose is not in its accustomed place but is instead parading around St. Petersburg in the form of a State Councillor.

A.F. Vel'tman's[27] "Alyonushka" is another interesting supernatural tale which contains everything from ghosts to animated broomsticks. The supernatural elements in this story are presented as parlor anecdotes.

In spite of the body of fantastic literature produced during the first decades of the nineteenth century, the problem posed in approaching, depicting, and motivating the supernatural has not received much attention in contemporary criticism. Soviet critics, of course, exhibit a certain bias in connection with this genre. They often attempt to negate the role of the supernatural altogether or isolate instead realistic currents which may be identified within these tales.

The majority of critics who will admit the existence of fantastic tales seem to consider their appearance in Russian literature a phenomenon which does not rate much attention. Bukhshtab, for example, denies the presence of the fantastic as a viable genre of the 1830's.[28] Pereverzev in an article about Vel'tman writes that fantasy is a game which the writer himself does not take seriously.[29] Stepanov admits the presence of what he terms the "fantastic-satiric tale," but he gives no analysis of this genre.[30] Sharoeva also writes about the fantastic short story, but she asserts the nonproductivity of this genre because it is not realistic.[31]

Western criticism of Russian literature of the supernatural is sparse. Bard discusses the supernatural in Russian literature and attempts to trace the origin of the supernatural elements in Pushkin, Zhukovskiy, A. Tolstoy, and others.[32] Ingham documents the presence of supernatural tales in Russian journals of the 1820's and early 1830's.[33]

Serious studies of the fantastic genre in Russian literature are few. An interesting article by Semibratova catalogues the critical material on Russian fantastic literature in an attempt to trace the various literary influences on the formation of fantastic prose in Russian fiction of this period. Semibratova finds the formation of fantastic prose in Russia conditioned by the Russian fairy tale, the fantasy novel of the eighteenth century, and translated fantastic tales and romances of the time.[34]

In an attempt to establish a typology of fantastic images Al'betkova also investigates Russian fantastic literature of the 1830's. Her survey includes not only the prose of Odoevskiy and Gogol' but also the poetry of Lermontov. Al'betkova distinguishes between grotesque fantasy and fantasy utilized in an attempt to resolve important philosophical issues. These types of fantasy she contrasts with realistic fantasy.[35]

Critics have devoted considerably more attention to the fantastic within the creativity of individual writers. The fantastic tales of Gogol' have received perhaps the most thorough critical evaluation. Annenskiy, for example, attempted to illuminate the problem of Gogol''s combination of fantasy with realism. Elements

10

of fantasy in "The Nose," "Viy," and "The Overcoat" are investigated. According to Annenskiy fantasy in Gogol''s works is utilized for an ethical purpose such as elucidation or examination. "The Nose" utilizes fantasy in order to heighten the comedy and unveil the banality of human life. "Viy" then represents an exegesis of fear: fear of strength and of the mysterious. According to Annenskiy, Gogol''s "Overcoat" proceeds beyond the level of elucidation to the area of judgment and condemnation.[36]

Another critic, Sipovskiy, proposes the division of the fantastic elements in Gogol''s Evenings on a Farm Near Dikanka according to their shades or nuances. This classification includes the comic fantasy of "The Night Before Christmas" the beautiful fantasy of "May Night," the grandiose fantasy of the hero-apparitions and the horrific fantasy of the sorcerer-wizard in "Terrible Revenge."[37] Gus, on the other hand, prefers to classify the fantastic elements in Gogol''s creativity as tragic, lyric, and humorous.[38]

Critics of Gogol''s creativity also attempt to rationalize the diversity of the fantastic elements within his works. Pospelov, for example, views the fantastic as a historical phenomenon. The diverse types of fantasy he explains as the introduction of various historical epochs during which there abounded a general belief in miracles and supernatural beings.[39] Stepanov asserts that the fantastic emerges as a means of comic depiction of morals and human disposition.[40] Gippius considers the contrast between fantasy and reality, the opposition between the mundane and the miraculous, as Gogol''s chief compositional intention.[41]

Gramzina introduces a more complex classification of Gogol''s fantasy. Her article is a development of the theme first introduced by Annenskiy. Gramzina, like Sipovskiy, distinguishes the shadings and nuances of fantasy as either comic or somber. She presents also a further classification of the fantastic as symbolic, mystical, and folkloristic. In an attempt to rationalize the fantastic elements in Gogol''s works not only as independent devices but also as a reflection of the reactionary attitudes of the writer himself, Gramzina attributes the comic fantasy to the ironic and satiric vein in Gogol''s creativity. The somber fantasy she equates with his mysticism, and the diversity of fantastic forms is linked with contradictions in the disposition of the writer himself.[42]

In perhaps the most enlightening criticism of Gogol''s fantasy Mann traces the evolution of Gogol''s technique from the time

11

of initial influence upon his creativity by the German romanticists. According to Mann, Gogol''s fantasy is delineated upon a temporal plan dependent upon whether the fantastic elements occurred in the past or take place in the present. The characteristic features of Gogolian fantasy would then be dependent upon the time of their occurrence. Mann delineates three successive epochs in the development of Gogol''s fantasy. According to the critic Gogol' first removed the carrier of fantasy into the past, leaving only the influence of the fantastic event in the present. Then he removed the carrier of the fantastic altogether, finally turning to reality and preserving only the nonfantastic. Fantasy then becomes linked with people's conduct, their way of life, of thinking and speaking.[43]

A number of critics have devoted articles also to the fantastic elements in various works of Pushkin. However, there exists no comprehensive study of the fantastic throughout Pushkin's entire creativity. Bocharov[44] and Gershenzon,[45] for example, have investigated the dreams in Pushkin's works. Shteyn in his comparative study of Pushkin and Hoffmann offers a chapter on the apparitions in the works of the two writers.[46] Ingham traces the origins of fantasy in "The Solitary Cottage" and "The Queen of Spades." A number of articles have been written in support or repudiation of the supernatural elements in "The Queen of Spades" and will be considered below.

Criticism dealing with fantastic elements in the creativity of other writers of the 1820's and 1830's is limited to passing references in monographs and occasional discussions of fantasy in particular works. Sakulin, for example, in a monograph on Odoevskiy underscores the writer's minimal preoccupation with the fantastic and indicates that this is a positive factor.[47] In an attempt to classify the fantastic elements in the works of Odoevskiy, Sakulin lists five basic types of fantasy: as external form; as a play of the imagination; fairy-tale fantasy; logical Utopian fantasy, and psychological fantasy.[48]

Bazanov, in studying the creativity of Bestuzhev, has noted the importance of folklore as a source of the author's treatment of the supernatural. Bazanov concludes that Bestuzhev's fantasy originates in popular folklore.[49] Leighton also presents a study of folkloristic elements in the fantasy of Bestuzhev's mature horror stories.[50]

The supernatural tale itself represents quite an extensive body of material which has not yet been subjected to thorough analysis. One of the primary aims of this study is simply to

12

bring to light these tales,many of which are unavailable to the English-speaking world. With this goal in mind we have translated all quoted materials into English. References, however, are to original Russian sources. Where transliteration is necessary, a system has been utilized which most closely approximates the English sounds of the original Russian letters.

We attempt to define this genre by determining the structure of the supernatural elements in these stories which, although rather complex, seem to conform to several uniform categories. The tale itself we define as the short form of epic narration which is anecdotal in structure and saturated with events. The supernatural tale is marked by elements which break free from commonly experienced reality and lead into the realm of the supernatural--i.e., phenomena above or superior to the recognized powers of nature. This includes manifestations of the spirit world (ghosts, infernal powers, animated corpses) and/or the relations between the "other world" and human beings.

In our study we attempt to determine the structure of these supernatural elements through examination of the fabric of the narrative itself. This includes the examination of factors which prefigure and motivate supernatural encounters. Of special importance is the role of the narrator and the point of view from which supernatural encounters are described.[51] We attempt also to indicate the various devices used by the authors to maintain, conceal, enhance or simply carry out the effect of the supernatural.

This is one method of tracing the development of a particular genre. Such a study leads directly to issues of a broader spectrum, namely toward an understanding of the evolution of Russian literature itself. Since many of these stories are quite obscure, we hope that this study will profit not only the serious student of literature but the specialist as well.

FOOTNOTES

[1] For an analysis of the supernatural in world literature see P. Penzoldt, The Supernatural in Fiction (New York: Humanities Press, 1965).

[2] A more complete outline of the development of the supernatural in world fiction is presented in H.P. Lovecraft, Supernatural Horror in Literature (New York: Dover Publications, 1973).

[3] "Nochnoe puteshestvie: Otryvok iz romana: Adventures of Hugh Trevor, by Thomas Holcraft," Biblioteque Britannique, Biblioteka dlya chteniya, (kn. 3, 1823), 81-99.

[4] Biblioteka dlya chteniya (10, 1823), 49-65.

[5] Bihlioteka dlya chteniya (8, 1823), 66-72.

[6] "Venden Castle" was published in 1823 in the periodical, Library for Reading; "Neygauzen Castle" appeared in 1824 in The Polar Star, and "Eyzen Castle" was published in the almanac Asterisk, in 1825.

[7] "The Traitor" first appeared in the periodical, Polar Star.

[8] "Son," Alsiona, Al'manakh na 1831 g. (kn. 1, 1831), 113-118.

[9] "Mogil'shchik," Girlanda (24-25, 1831), 188-189.

[10] "Oboroten', ili starukha-krasavitsa, narodnaya russkaya skazka," Novosti literaturi (kn. 13, 1825), 1-14.

[11] O. Somov, "Oboroten'," Podsnezhnik, al'manakh na 1829 g. (Saint Petersburg, 1829), 189-191.

[12] Syn otechestva (6, 1832).

[13] Damskiy zhurnal (10, 1831), 145-151.

[14] Moskovskiy telegraf, ch. 50 (8, 1833), 574.

[15] _Moskovskiy vestnik_, ch. 10 (14, 1828), 160.

[16] Scott's article may be found in _Lives of Eminent Drama-tists_ (London, 1887), 551-578.

[17] The original appeared in _The Foreign Quarterly Review_ (July, 1827), 60-98.

[18] Anton Pogorel'skiy was the pseudonym of Aleksey Alek-seevich Perovskiy (1787-1836), an early Russian romantic writer. Educated at Moscow University, Pogorel'skiy participated in the War of 1812 and afterward served in the Ministry of Education. His tale of the Lafyortov poppy-seed-cake lady enjoyed great pop-ularity and received the enthusiastic praise of Pushkin himself. In 1828 Pogorel'skiy published a two-part collection entitled _The Double or My Evenings in the Ukraine_, fantastic tales heavily in-fluenced by E.T.A. Hoffmann. In 1829 he published a children's fairy tale "The Black Chicken or the Subterranean Dwellers." Pogorel'skiy's only novel, _The Monastery Girl_ (1830-1833), de-picts the Ukrainian gentry in a rather humorous light. The author is probably best remembered, however, for his delightful tales which are a delicate mixture of fantasy and reality.

[19] Orest Mikhailovich Somov (1793-1833) was a Russian lit-erary critic, writer, and journalist. Born into a family of Ukrainian gentry, he was educated at Kharkov University and in 1817 journeyed to St. Petersburg where he became acquainted with the future leaders of the abortive Decembrist Uprising of 1825. Soon after his arrival in the Capital, Somov became a mem-ber of the _Free Society of the Lovers of Russian Literature_ and the _Free Society of Lovers of Literature, Science, and the Arts_. In 1823 he published a tract entitled "On Romantic Poetry" in which he asserted that the basis for an independent Russian contribution to the romantic movement lay in an emphasis upon Russian history, ethnography and popular language, and he re-nounced what he termed the "elegaic" spirit of contemporary European romanticism. After the Decembrist revolt Somov was arrested but was freed for lack of evidence. From 1825-1832 he participated in the publication of the almanac _Northern Flowers_, and in 1830-31 he served as the editor of the _Literary Gazette_. In his literary works Somov, who was considered a precursor of Gogol', strove to preserve his Ukrainian heritage. This ethno-graphic preoccupation is inherent in such stories as "The Evil Eye" and "Kievan Witches." He also produced several Russian fairy tales such as "The Tale of the Bone-Breaking Bear and Ivan the Merchant's Son" and "In the Field Birth Doesn't Count." His last tales, "Matchmaking" and "Mommie and her Little Son,"

are less romantic in spirit and adhere more carefully to the depiction of real life and human psychology. Although Somov receives little critical attention and is usually considered a secondary writer, his work in the area of the literary language is truly innovative. In the future he may well rise to his true place in the Pantheon of first-rate Russian writers.

[20]"The Monster" appeared in Northern Flowers for 1830, and "A command from the Other World" was published in Literary Museum for 1827.

[21]Skaz is a Russian word which indicates narration by someone other than the author directly. Vivid language, colloquialisms and slang are often employed which provide a more complete characterization of the fictitious narrator.

[22]Aleksandr Aleksandrovich Bestuzhev (1797-1837) was a well-known Russian writer of the early nineteenth century whose works were published under the name of A. Marlinskiy. An officer in the guards, Bestuzhev was stationed in the town of Marll from which he came to derive his authorial pseudonym. In 1822 Bestuzhev met Kondratiy Ryleev with whom he collaborated from 1823-1825 as editor-publisher of the popular literary almanac Polar Star, a journal which was to express the romantic point of view in Russian literature. In 1823 Bestuzhev was recruited by Ryleev into the Northern Society of the Decembrist organization. As one of the leaders of the society's radical left wing, he participated in the uprising of 1825, for which he was arrested and imprisoned in Petersburg and in Finland. Bestuzhev was to spend the rest of his life either incarcerated in Siberia or in forced military service in the Caucasus region. In 1830 he returned to literature and began to publish in the literary journals a succession of romantic prose tales which made the name Marlinskiy a household word in Russia. Writing prodigiously from 1830-1836, he turned out various historical and society stories as well as tales and travelogues. In addition to his many romantic tales Bestuzhev produced the novels Ammalat-Bek (1832) and Mullah-Nur (1835-1836), which were set in the Caucasus. Suffering a fate typical of his romantic heroes, Bestuzhev was killed in battle with Circassian tribesmen in 1837. His way of life and literary style dominated the literary milieu of the early 1830's and came to be known as "Marlinism."

[23]"An Evening at the Caucasian Waters" appeared in the periodical Son of the Fatherland and Northern Archive in 1830. "The Terrible Divination" was published in The Moscow Telegraph in 1831, and "The Cuirassier" appeared in Son of the Fatherland in 1832.

[24]Prince Vladimir Fyodorovich Odoevskiy (1803-1869) was a Russian writer, journalist and philosopher of the mid-nineteenth century. Educated in Moscow, Odoevskiy moved to St. Petersburg where he worked in the Department of Spiritual Affairs and served on the editorial board of various journals. While still a youth he became one of the most visible members of the Society of the Lovers of Wisdom, a group of romantics who followed the teachings of the German philosopher Schelling. In 1824-1825 Odoevskiy, together with his friend V.K. Kyukhel'beker, published the almanac Mnemosina, which agitated for the creation of a truly independent Russian literature. Odoevskiy acted also as a music critic who championed the creation of a Russian national school of music stemming from the composer Glinka. In addition he wrote a number of scientific books and articles for the general public on problems of education. Odoevskiy also wrote a number of fairy tales and tales for children. Best known of his works in the West is Russian Nights, a series of philosophical conversations critical of western European culture and influence in Russia.

[25]Aleksandr Sergeevich Pushkin (1799-1837) is Russia's most beloved poet. Young Pushkin began to write verse while still a student at the famous lyceum in Tsarskoe Selo, an institution established by the Tsar for children of the nobility. Upon graduation he entered the civil service but fell into difficulties with the police after writing political poems and epigrams. In 1820 Pushkin was exiled from the Capital and was sent to the South. Here he wrote what was to become his first important work, the fairy tale "Ruslan and Lyudmila". It was in the South that he began the well-known novel in verse Eugene Onegin. Pushkin's southern exile probably prevented him from taking an active part in the Decembrist Uprising of 1825. He was arrested on suspicion and brought before the Tsar who promised to become his personal censor, an honor which proved to be of dubious value. After 1830 Pushkin began to write prose and study history. Stemming from this period were the Tales of Belkin (1830) publication of the play Boris Godunov (1831), "The Queen of Spades" (1834), and the only full-sized novel written and published during Pushkin's lifetime, The Captain's Daughter (1836). In 1836 Pushkin founded the liberal literary journal The Contemporary. In 1837 the great poet was mortally wounded in a duel with the Baron Georges d'Anthes, a Frenchman in Russian service, who allegedly had made improper advances toward Pushkin's wife. Pushkin's contribution to Russian literature is many-sided. Perhaps most important is the precision and naturalness of his language which was to influence entire generations of Russian writers who were to follow. Today also Pushkin's verses are memorized and recited by millions of Russians who honor his memory by laying flowers at the many Pushkin monuments throughout the U.S.S.R.

[26]Nikolay Vasil'evich Gogol' (1809-1852) was a Russian prose writer of the first magnitude. Born and raised in the Ukraine, he came from a family of minor gentry origin. Like many others he soon travelled to the Capital and joined the civil service. Dissatisfied with his position as a minor clerk, Gogol' turned his energies toward literature. His first successful collection of tales, Evenings on a Farm Near Dikanka, appeared in 1831-1832, followed in 1835 by new collections entitled Mirgorod and Arabesques. Gogol' served for one year as a professor of history at the University of St. Petersburg but soon became disenchanted and resigned his position. In 1836 he published the immensely successful play The Inspector General, a case of mistaken identity concerning the foibles of city officials who expect their nemesis in the form of a government inspector. Also in 1836 Gogol' left Russia for Italy where he was to spend the next twelve years. It was there were he worked on his great masterpiece, Dead Souls (1842), which is the tale of a civil servant who travels about Russia attempting a massive swindle by buying up dead serfs whose names are still on the tax lists. Also in 1842 Gogol' produced perhaps his most famous short story, "The Overcoat." Seemingly haunted by moral and religious problems, he returned to Russia in 1852, destroyed the manuscript of the second part of Dead Souls and literally starved himself to death. Gogol' possessed a great gift for caricature. He was Russia's greatest humorist and at the same time ironically was his country's greatest practitioner of the horror story.

[27]Aleksandr Fomich Vel'tman (1800-1870) was a Russian poet, novelist, and short story writer of the mid-nineteenth century. Born into a family of impoverished nobility, he was educated both in Moscow and St. Petersburg. In 1817 Vel'tman completed training as a military topographer and was sent to Bessarabia. In Kishinyov he became acquainted with Pushkin. He also developed an interest in the archeology of the southern region. As a result of this interest Vel'tman later published a number of archeological and historical works on this area of the country. In 1842 he became an assistant to the director of the Armory and he himself became its director in 1852. Vel'tman's literary career began in 1828 when he began publishing poems in various literary journals. His first successful literary effort was the novel The Wanderer (1831-1832), the story of the author's journey though the imagination. Vel'tman also wrote a series of historical novels including The Immortal Kashchey (1833), The Lunatic (1834), and Svyatoslavich, the Hostile Pupil (1835). In 1846 Vel'tman published Salomey, the first of a cycle of novels entitled Adventures Drawn from the Sea of Life. In his works Vel'tman combines fantasy and reality, adventure tales with accounts of everyday life. Because of his predilection for melodrama and this tendency to intertwine fantasy with reality Vel'tman has been called a precursor of Dostoevskiy. Even during

his own lifetime Vel'tman's popularity waned, and he has remained untranslated and relatively unknown in the West.

[28] B. Ya. Bukhshtab, "Pervye romany Vel'tmana," Russkaya proza, V. Eykhenbaum and Ya. Tynyanov, eds. (Leningrad, 1926), 205.

[29] V.F. Pereverzev, Iz istokov russkogo realisticheskogo romana (Moscow, 1965), 114.

[30] N.L. Stepanov, "Povest' 30-kh godov," Starinnaya povest' (Leningrad, 1929), 22.

[31] T.G. Sharoeva, "Russkaya povest' kontsa 20-kh-nachala 30-kh godov," Doklady AnAzSSR (2, 1958), 185.

[32] Joseph Bard, "The Supernatural in Russian Literature," Essays by Divers Hands (London, 1960), 68-84.

[33] N.W. Ingham, "E.T.A. Hoffmann in Russia, 1822-1845," Doctoral Dissertation (Harvard University, 1963), 348-356.

[34] I.V. Semibratova, "K istorii voprosa o russkoy fantasticheskoy proze 30-kh godov XIX veka," Vestnik moskovskogo universiteta (4, 1972), 18-28.

[35] R.I. Al'betkova, "Fantasticheskie obrazy v russkom romantizme 30-kh godov XIX veka," Iz istorii russkogo romantizma. Sbornik statey (Kemerovo: 1971), 86-100.

[36] I. Annenskiy, "Forma fantasticheskogo u Gogolya," Russkaya shkola (10, 1890), 93-104.

[37] V.V. Sipovskiy, Istoriya russkoy slovesnosti, ch. 3, vyp. I (Saint Petersburg, 1911), 143.

[38] M. Gus, Gogol' i nikolaevskaya Rossiya (Moscow, 1957), 61.

[39] G.N. Pospelov, Tvorchestvo N.V. Gogolya (Moscow, 1953), 43.

[40] N.L. Stepanov, N.V. Gogol': Tvorcheskiy put' (Moscow, 1959), 78.

[41]V.V. Gippius, Ot Pushkina do Bloka (Moscow-Leningrad, 1966), 96.

[42]T. Gramzina, "Vidy fantasticheskogo v tvorchestve Gogol-ya," Uchyonie zapiski kirgizskogo gosudarstvennogo universiteta, vyp. 5, Slavyanskiy sbornik (Frunze), 125.

[43]Yu.V. Mann, "Evolyutsiya gogolevskoy fantastiki," K istorii russkogo romantizma (Moscow, 1973), 219-255.

[44]S.G. Bocharov, "O smysle 'Grobovshchika'," Kontekst - 1873. Literaturno-teoreticheskie issledovaniya (Moscow, 1974), 196-230.

[45]M.O. Gershenzon, "Sny Pushkina," Stat'i o Pushkine, Istoriya i teoriya iskusstv. Vyp. I (Moscow, 1926), 96-110.

[46]S. Shteyn, Pushkin i Gofman: Sravnitel'noe literaturnoe issledovanie (Derpt, 1927), 203-255.

[47]P.N. Sakulin, Iz istorii russkogo idealizma. Knyaz' V.F. Odoevskiy (Moscow, 1913), 290.

[48]V.G. Bazanov, Ocherki dekabristskoy literatury (Moscow, 1953), 375.

[49]Ibid.

[50]L. Leighton, "Aleksandr Bestuzhev-Marlinskiy: The Romantic Prose Tale in Russia," Doctoral Dissertation, (University of Wisconsin, 1968), 206-239.

[51]For an exhaustive study of the role of point of view in literature see B. Uspensky, A Poetics of Composition, (Berkeley: University of California Press, 1973).

CHAPTER TWO

THE SUPERNATURAL DREAM

Where does man better articulate his fantasy than in the dream, a state in which guilt finds expiation and unfulfilled psychological needs are realized? Writers have long exploited the myriad of possibilities linked with this most tenuous aspect of human experience. Depicting the supernatural as a dream is probably the simplest method of constructing a fantastic tale and may be traced to the earliest Russian stories of this type. Russian writers, who have treated the supernatural dream both seriously and comically, have invented a number of interesting devices which mask the dream from the reader and heighten the element of mystery contained within the story itself.

Often an act of fainting or simply falling asleep is removed from the story line, and the reader does not realize that the hero is asleep or unconscious. Indeed, the author may exert great effort in order to conceal this fact from the reader who may be very surprised to learn that the hero was only dreaming. Another device is the obliterated awakening in which the hero allegedly awakens early in the story. Because of this the reader does not believe that the ensuing tale is in reality a dream. At the close of the story the incredulous reader discovers that this early awakening was itself a part of the dream sequence.

Typical Russian tales which contain supernatural dreams are Odoevskiy's "Brigadier," "A Corpse's Mockery," and "The Live Corpse"; Bestuzhev's "Terrible Divination"; and Pushkin's "Undertaker." Structurally simple and a story of relatively short duration, Odoevskiy's "Brigadier"[1] consists of three basic segments, motivation for the appearance of a talking corpse, the corpse's sermonizing, and the effect of all this upon the hero-narrator.

The moralistic tone of this story is established at the onset by the epigraph concerning the utter insignificance of a certain unlucky fellow:

> He had lived and lived--and the only thing
> that remained of him was the newspaper an-
> nouncement that he had 'left for Rostov'.[2]

This moralizing continues as the narrator reports that he had been present at the deathbed of one who had died:

> leaving nothing behind, nary a thought, not
> a single feeling.[3]

The wretched fellow, it seems:

was loved by no one and loved no one.[4]

It is the image of his friend's corpse, washed, shaved, and in its uniform that arouses within the narrator unnatural and heightened feelings:

Thoughts and feelings were crowded in my
soul. . .For a long time they churned like
magic vapors.[5]

The narrator has now sunk into a dreamy hallucinatory state conducive to an encounter with the other world:

And at last, little by little, the image of the
deceased formed before me. And it was exactly as if he were alive. He pointed out his
abdominal cavity and gazed at me intently with
his expressionless eyes.[6]

The appearance of this corpse is linked initially with the sense of sight as the apparition bares its abdominal cavity while staring at the incredulous hero. The deceased is then manifest audibly through mocking and haughty laughter. Finally the corpse makes itself evident to the narrator's sense of touch by grasping his hand, and the frightened hero is thwarted in various attempts to evade the apparition which follows him unceasingly. Such a scene is, of course, reminiscent of the depiction of a nightmare.

The ensuing remarks of the corpse typify the use of the supernatural in connection with the presentation of a moral lesson. Initially, the corpse-apparition speaks concerning the necessity that sympathy and pity be extended to those who have led barren lives and have engendered no love within others. A second tirade concerns the unfortunate upbringing of the deceased and motivates his life of ineptitude, uselessness, and his dearth of spiritual values. There follows a review of the corpse's youth, unhappy marriage, poor family life, final illness, and death. The entire lesson concludes with the corpse's remark:

And my whole life was presented before me in
all of its loathsome nakedness![7]

The grotesque horror of death is reemphasized in the final appearance of the dead man's bloody tears, and the transition to reality is marked by the simple statement:

And he disappeared with a sad smile.[8]

The narrator now reports that he fell on his knees, wept, and prayed for a rather lengthy period. This serves to underscore the change brought about in one whose inability to experience deep emotion has now been overcome by the appearance of his friend from beyond the grave.

The tale is constructed as a first person narrative maintained initially by the hero-narrator and then from the point of view of the corpse. The state of mind of the narrator whose emotions are aroused after he has attended the funeral of his friend motivates the supernatural dream sequence. This dream is not hidden from the reader, and the story maintains a continual forward movement, with the dream itself separated only by elipses in the text. There is no description of the hero's return to reality or of any intermediary state between complete consciousness and sleep. The corpse is manifest visually, audibly, and tangibly, and leaves the hero in a new state of heightened awareness and sensitivity. The supernatural encounter exists solely for the author's expression of a moral--the inevitability of death and the necessity for proper conduct within human relationships.

"A Corpse's Mockery,"[9] also by Odoevskiy, is more complex in the deployment of the supernatural. Segments of this tale include an initial passage on weather conditions, the heroine's eerie drive to a ball, her subsequent hallucination and altered conduct as a result of the fantastic dream.

The initial description of an environment energized by an autumnal storm establishes the scene for an encounter with the world beyond. The raging storm, a surging river bursting from its banks, swaying lanterns, and darting shadows are linked with general agitation in the city where the young heroine is traveling. Human activity is elevated to a frenetic state--a condition conducive to occurrences of the supernatural. The young woman is thoroughly terrified by the waves of the enraged river and by the fierce howling wind. The nocturnal atmosphere, illumined by torch bearers in a funeral procession, further agitates the young heroine's state of mind.

Initial manifestation of the corpse-apparition is visual and is constructed from the point of view of the woman:

It seemed to her that the corpse raised its blue
face and gazed at her with that motionless smile
with which the dead mock the living.[10]

The heroine's reaction to this corpse is depicted externally with
the narrator's statements that the frightened woman gasped and
pressed herself against the carriage wall. The narrator does not
himself see the ghost but merely describes the reactions of the
heroine. This is intended to strengthen the reader's impression
that the entire episode is a psychological phenomenon in the mind
of a receptive victim. An authorial digression now explains the
previous relationship between the young lady and the deceased.
The author's message is introduced at this point and assumes the
form of an attack upon marriages of convenience, underscoring
the guilt of the young woman who had spurned her true love,
the unfortunate fellow in the casket.

The young lady is pale, trembling and barely able to make
her way up the marble steps into the ballroom. Her husband's
wooden hand further reminds the heroine of her deceased lover
whose hand would tighten convulsively when touching her own.
These descriptive elements motivate and foreshadow the fainting
scene which is now to follow and initiate yet another supernatural encounter.

The act of fainting is removed from the narrative which allegedly flows forward with no pause. The reader does not perceive the actions which follow as parts of the heroine's rather
elaborate hallucination. The scene instead proceeds with the
simple statement:

A noise was heard. . .[11]

Events occurring henceforth form the young heroine's dream.
This hallucination is presented initially from her point of view:

The young beauty saw that some of the guests
were whispering among themselves. Others
quickly ran out of the room and returned
trembling.[12]

A call for water, which in reality occurs in order to revive the
heroine, is instead perceived by her as part of a dream. The
moment of encounter within this fantasy is perceived tangibly by
the young woman as the corpse's head touches her own, and cold
drops from its waxen face fall upon her. This tactile perception
is enforced visually as the terrified heroine follows the corpse's
dumbstruck eyes, reproachful and mocking. Horrific laughter is

heard, and the hallucination ends with the grotesque corpse calling out the young woman's name.

The victim of this hallucination is now seen once more in full possession of her senses:

> When Liza came to she was lying on her bed.
> The sun's rays gilded the green curtain. In
> a long armchair yawning angrily, her husband
> was conversing with the doctor. [13]

It is only at this moment that the reader understands the true nature of these events which were a hallucination experienced by the impressionable young heroine during a fainting spell. The doctor's lengthy explanation of this hallucination provides psychological motivation for the fainting fit, and the story ends with a description of the heroine's conduct one year after this terrifying episode. Her life has not changed, and she still prefers the false conventions of high society. Encounters with the corpse of her now long-forgotten lover have not affected the superficial society girl, but the perceptions of the reader rise to a new level, a recognition of retribution for evil and responsibility for one's actions.

As can be seen, this story is provided with supernatural elements which are introduced chiefly for the sake of expressing a moral lesson, eventual punishment for the evils of society life. Occurrences of the supernatural are justified by environmental shading and frenetic motion (flitting shadows, energetic dancing, and raging water). The heroine's fantastic dream is thoroughly motivated psychologically and is depicted only from her point of view with a grotesque corpse manifest visually, audibly, and tangibly. The entire scene becomes all the more horrific since the heroine's fainting spell is masked from the reader, who only in retrospect understands that the episode is merely a hallucinatory dream. The illusion of reality is maintained since the narrative proceeds without interruption into the dream sequence, the events of which are obliterated retrospectively, and the normal flow of events is reestablished with the protagonist's return to a conscious state.

Odoevskiy's "The Live Corpse"[14] represents yet another version of the supernatural dream-tale in which the hero, Vasiliy Kuzmich, awakens beyond the grave and secretly witnesses how friends and loved ones react to his demise. This eavesdropping ghost follows the activities of his carousing servants and drops in on his friends who are more concerned with eating and drinking than with thoughts of sadness at his death. Vasiliy's former girlfriend is caught in an assignation with someone else, and a second girlfriend is snoring as if nothing had happened. The corpse also observes the machinations of his sons in their attempts to disinherit a niece. Unable to follow these scenes of indifference, corruption, and deception, Vasiliy is about to return to the grave when he awakens from what is now presented as a dream.

The epigraph, a reminder that no single action or word of man is forgotten, that each man is responsible for his most insignificant action, establishes the moral tone of the narrative. The supernatural encounters are structured so as to illustrate this didactic message. Within this tale we find a device which we shall term an "obliterated awakening." The hero, Vasiliy, awakens early in the story, and the reader believes that the events which follow are factual. At the close of the tale the protagonist awakens once more, and the earlier awakening is placed in perspective as a portion of the dream sequence itself. As a result the dream is successfully masked, and for a time the reader is inclined toward belief in the supernatural.

The plot of this tale is a variation on the theme of the corpse who pays a call upon the living. This particular corpse-apparition, however, is not apparent to those whom he observes. The first person narration is conducted from the point of view of the ghost, with the narrative proceeding from a vantage point external to the characters themselves whose actions and words alone are evident. Their thoughts and psychological reactions must be deduced by the reader. Scenes of encounters with mortals are interspersed with interpretive comment from the point of view of the ghost-narrator. Each episode illustrates the theme of the protagonist's responsibility for the evil which he has sown in the world. On the other side of the grave Vasiliy fully recognizes the hypocrisy and deception of the world from which he has emerged.

Odoevskiy was not the only Russian writer to create supernatural tales which contain fantastic dreams. Bestuzhev's "The Terrible Divination,"[15] for example, contains a supernatural dream as well as anecdotal accounts of the supernatural. Structural disassembly of this tale reveals the following segments: (1) the hero-narrator's confession of his illicit love affair and decision to attend a ball given by his lover; (2) the narrator's journey to this ball, the supernatural anecdotes of his driver and their subsequent loss of orientation in a snowstorm; (3) the accidental stop at a village New Year's gathering, accompanying anecdotes, and the appearance of a mysterious stranger; (4) the divination scene; (5) the hero's fantastic dream and (6) the awakening and revelation of his changed conduct as a result of this fantastic occurrence.

The narrator's confession of his passionate love affair indicates his agitated frame of mind and presents the initial motivating circumstance for the subsequent plunge into fantasy. Depiction of events prior to the dream sequence provides psychological motivation for the protagonist's encounter with the supernatural.

Drawn to the ball by horses which race like a whirlwind, the hero imagines that he visualizes the ballroom guests involved in frenzied dancing. Such agitated and frenetic motion is an additional link in the chain of events leading to the eventual manifestation of supernatural phenomena.

Environmental coloration provides further supernatural shading. Clumps of spruce are depicted:

like corpses, wrapped in snowy shrouds, as
if stretching out their frozen arms to us.[16]

The coachman's stories of water nymphs and werewolves strengthen the supernatural atmosphere of the sleigh ride. Further supernatural hues are provided by the anecdotes narrated at the New Year's gathering which is interrupted by the narrator and his guide. The sudden appearance of a mysterious stranger who does not cross himself before the icons lends an eerie aspect to the gathering and further impresses the hero. Thus the protagonist's fantastic dream is carefully foreshadowed.

The moment that the hero drifts into unconsciousness is removed from the text, and the dream proceeds without the reader's awareness, commencing with the inebriated diviner's remark:

He is coming! He is coming![17]

The narrative now continues from a first person orientation, and the dream remains completely masked, serving outwardly as a simple linear continuation of the previous plot movement.

Description of the mysterious stranger throughout the dream sequence is consistent with the previous treatment of this character who is subject both to supernatural and earthly origin. The stranger is depicted as appearing suddenly and almost supernaturally to announce that the husband of the hero's lover Pauline is searching for them both. This stranger seems privy to information which could only have been obtained through supernatural means, yet he is able to explain away all this knowledge rationally. The narrator, however, remains unconvinced, and his suspicions are betrayed in the remark:

Are you a devil or a human being?[18]

31

Supernatural environmental shading is also maintained throughout the dream sequence. The nocturnal assignation between the hero and Pauline is accomplished in an old domestic theater illuminated by moonlight which casts the stage in an eerie spectrum. The narrator admits his frenzied state of mind at the prospect of a secret tryst with his beloved and reports that he trembled as if in a fever. This feverish and frenetic state of mind combined with the influence of the environment unite to provide motivation for the fantastic events which follow.

A frantic chase over the snowy countryside is followed by a clash between the hero and the rather antagonistic husband, the subsequent murder of the latter, and disposal of the corpse. The mysterious stranger is continually described as half human and half devil whose hellish laughter is linked with attempts to thrust the unsuspecting hero into an infernal grave.

The hero's return to conscious reality is constructed so as to blend carefully into the continuing narrative without an abrupt break in the linear movement of the text. An oppressive force which prevents him from forming the sign of the Cross during the fateful plunge into a hellish grave is now revealed as his heavy bearskin fur coat. Return to awareness is linked also with the presence of positive supernatural forces which negate the hero's misfortune and bring about a rapid return to reality.

The hero's return to a conscious state is also marked by the exclamations:

Where am I? What's happened to me?[19]

The final outcome of the story consists of the hero's description of the surrounding graveyard, his remarks on the seeming reality of the dream, and indications of the effect that the supernatural dream had upon his life--in essence, that he gave his word of honor never to see Pauline again and kept it. The narrator's final didactic message indicates that the tale is the allegorical embodiment of a moral.

This tale, like others of its type, follows a prescribed pattern in the construction of supernatural elements. A frenzied state of mind and eerie environmental coloration form psychological motivation for the hero's fantastic dream. The mysterious stranger-devil is subject to dual interpretation and is not definitely rationalized either as a supernatural being or as a mortal. Christian supernatural forces which are linked with the protagonist's return to consciousness are not manifest physically, but their influence is apparent.

The dream sequence is effectively masked from the reader and is obliterated through the absence of a break in the narrative at the point where the hero lapses into unconsciousness. Within the dream sequence itself the first person narrative is maintained as are supernatural environmental coloration and ambiguous description of the mysterious devil figure. The hero's return to reality is also carefully integrated into the narrative and is manifest without any abrupt transition. The final outcome reveals the author's didactic message by indicating that the hero's changed conduct is the result of his fantastic dream.

The supernatural dream-tale which presents perhaps the greatest interest because of its structural complexity and comic-horrific alternation is Pushkin's "The Undertaker."[20] Adrian Prokorov, the undertaker, is invited to a feast hosted by his new neighbor, the German shoemaker Gottlieb Schultz, who is celebrating his wedding anniversary. Many local craftsmen are in attendance at this gathering, and all drink to the health of their "clients." Having imbibed too heavily, the undertaker returns home announcing that he will invite his past customers to a housewarming party. During the night the unfortunate Prokorov dreams that his former clients terrorize him by appearing unshaven in their graveclothes, dancing and wracking their bones.

This story may be disassembled into four structural components. The initial situation, Prokorov's move to a new residence, serves to introduce the undertaker and his daughter and casts light upon the disposition of Prokorov, by habit a rather morose and gloomy old fellow who is scheming to obtain the business of burying old Tryukhina, a merchant's wife who has been on the brink of the grave for over a year. Within the tale's second section this situation is developed and contains the acceptance of the shoemaker's invitation as well as the scene at the wedding anniversary celebration where the jesting toasts are proposed. This segment is a comic alternation which leads into and provides realistic motivation for the dream sequence which is to follow. The third segment contains the introduction of the fantastic element during which Prokorov is visited by many of his former customers in the form of animated corpses or skeletons. This particular section is formed realistically with a certain admixture of the horrific. Finally, the fantastic visitation is revealed as a dream, a twist of plot which brings the narrative to a close.

A somber tone of narration is established initially by the epigraph from Derzhavin:

Do we not each day behold coffins, the grey
hairs of our aging universe?[21]

Immediate comic alternation, however, is evident in the humorous description of a scraggy pair of horses dragging themselves along. The narrator himself lends further comic spirit with his remark concerning those who have the misfortune or "pleasure" of utilizing the services of an undertaker. Also of humorous note is the bootmaker's absurd comment that a corpse cannot "live" without a coffin. These jesting remarks followed by the comic description of the wedding anniversary celebration with its plethora of toasts places the narrative into a comic vein. The humorous description of this anniversary party serves structurally as an alternation of tone from the somber initiation of the narrative and also motivates the episode which is to become Prokorov's dream. Intoxication here serves as a motivating device for the supernatural event as a hallucination.

The dream sequence is treated realistically and is integrated into the story in such a way that the reader does not realize that Prokorov is experiencing a dream. Realistic motivation for the undertaker's dream and subsequent encounter with the supernatural as the result of heavy imbibing is provided by the narrator's remark that beer flowed freely. The artisans' subsequent toasts to their clients form a psychological impression in the old undertaker's mind. This imprint is underscored by Prokorov's offense at the suggestion that his trade may not be as honorable as the crafts of others. Final impetus for the dream is provided by Prokorov's drunken assertion that he will invite his clients to a housewarming.

Prokorov's dream now proceeds and remains unannounced within the text which provides no indication of the transfer from the real world to the protagonist's dream state. This transformation is completely realistic and is masked from the reader with the words:

> Outside it was still dark when Adrian was awakened.[22]

Further realistic framework is supplied by the description of the dead woman, yellow as wax, surrounded by burning candles, with priests chanting prayers, and the undertaker preparing for the funeral.

As some critics point out, the narrative now becomes less subjective with the disappearance of the omniscient narrator who also does not know that a dream has begun. As the dream continues the formerly jocular narrator, who seems to know so much about world literature and also about the personal lives of the undertaker and his German friends, is not present. During the dream sequence the narrator actually emerges in only one remark:

By the Church of the Ascension our friend
Yurko hailed him and, recognizing the undertaker, he wished him a good night.[23]

The tendency is now for the dream to incline toward the point of
view of the undertaker.

Initial supernatural shading is accomplished by linking the
undertaker's fantastic encounter with religious ritual. The undertaker, for example, vows:

I'll call back those I've worked on, the
Christian corpses.[24]

This remark is immediately followed by the old servant's fearful
exclamation:

Cross yourself![25]

an expression which implies the presence of evil forces.

The development of an atmosphere of mystery also leads into
and underscores the supernatural occurrence. This mystery begins when the undertaker approaches his new home and encounters two enigmatic figures. The initial appearance of these unknown strangers is realistic, and Prokorov suspects that they
may be robbers. Identification of the visitors comes suddenly
with the narrator's laconic remark:

The room was filled with corpses.[26]

The initial appearance of these visitors from the other world is
rendered from Prokorov's point of view:

The undertaker was already approaching his
home when suddenly it seemed to him that
someone approached his gate, opened it and
disappeared.[27]

Further perception of the corpses is described also from the
point of view of the undertaker:

It seemed to Adrian that people were walking
about his rooms.[28]

Depiction of these animated corpses is both horrific and comic.
The yellow and blue faces, sunken mouths, dim half-closed eyes
and protruding noses of the corpses which bow amiably at the

undertaker form a grotesque scene. However, the realistic horror of these guests from beyond is extenuated by the narrator's
reference to the visitors as "honorable" company. Also serving
to balance this horrific presentation is the image of several
corpses addressing Prokorov in the familiar form and announcing
their pleasure in responding to his invitation.

A second example of horrific-comic alternation within this
dream sequence is the appearance of Pyotr Petrovich, a grotesque skeleton, which is depicted as smiling tenderly at Prokorov and extending its bony arms to the undertaker in a sign
of affectionate embrace. The corpse's reminder that Prokorov
had misrepresented in the sale of its coffin indicates that Prokorov's sense of guilt may have played a role in the scene con-
jured up because of the undertaker's drunken stupor. Later
after the protests of other corpses, the undertaker is so filled
with horror that he falls unconscious. As a result the supernatural event is associated with the hero's aroused mental state and
ensuing lapse into unconsciousness.

The narrative now comes to a rapid conclusion with a rational explanation for the supernatural visitation as a part of Prokorov's fantastic dream. The servant also explains that the tai-
lor and policeman have called to invite Prokorov to another party.
This motivates the presence of the two mysterious figures who
initiate the undertaker's fantastic encounter, and once more reality itself is found to be the source of the supernatural.

The undertaker's fantastic dream has stimulated a variety of
critical activity in the work of such Russian scholars as Gershenzon, Bocharov, and Eykhenbaum. Gershenzon, for example, investigates the dream in Pushkin's creativity before 1833.[29] He
correctly underscores the prophetic nature of these dreams (Ot-
rep'ev sees himself falling from a tower in "Boris Godunov";
Mar'ya Gavrilovna sees Vladimir dead in "The Snowstorm"; and
Tat'yana sees Onegin as the murderer of Lenskiy in Eugene
Onegin). Gershenzon notes the deeply hidden psychological
motivational factors which are present in these dreams, all of
which are separated from the preceding events and are connected prophetically with the future.

Prokorov's dream, however, should be differentiated from
the others within Pushkin's creativity because the undertaker's
dream is excluded from the real action of the story. This is
Bocharov's main conclusion, that the dream in Prokorov's case
remains disconnected from events which follow and is also effectively removed from the life of the undertaker who remains
unaffected by this encounter with the supernatural. The dream
is not prophetic as far as the events in Prokorov's life are
concerned since Tryukhina does not really·die. However, the

dream is prophetic as far as it reflects the present psychological state of the undertaker even though the condition remains unacknowledged by Prokorov himself. The decisive effect of "The Undertaker" lies in the fact that the fantastic events of the dream are removed from the temporal flow of the narrative. Yet in another sense these fantastic events remain as an integral portion of the psychological portrayal of the undertaker himself.[30]

Eykhenbaum also underscores the importance of the narrative reversal engendered by Prokorov's fantastic dream. Such narrative reversions are typical of many Pushkin tales, and one may consider this inversion the chief characteristic feature and constructive principle of Pushkin's tale.[31]

Thus it may be said that "The Undertaker" is a tale in which comic, realistic, and horrific scenes alternate. The problem of mystery is effectively handled through obliteration of the dream sequence, and final motivation for the fantastic is presented only retrospectively. Occurrences of the supernatural are predicated upon an atmosphere of suspense and horror. The supernatural is coupled with religious ritual, and supernatural phenomena are experienced by a single individual who is in an intensified emotional state, leading into a lapse of consciousness at the conclusion of the transnormal event. Intoxication is presented as a possible motivation for the fantastic dream as a hallucination. Felicitous ghosts appearing to a solemn mortal in fact forms a situational reverse of the conventional ghost story. In the final analysis, "The Undertaker" must be considered a parody on the traditional supernatural tale.

Pushkin's tale and other supernatural dream tales are subject to similar patterns of construction. The most predominant distinctive feature of this story type is a link between the supernatural dream and some moral truth. This didactic message is usually expressed through an attack upon hypocrisy in society and the assertion of the necessity for moral conduct in everyday life. In this connection the appearance of supernatural beings is motivated largely by the guilt of the protagonist who has not lived as he should.

Construction of the dream sequence itself also follows similar patterns. Initially the dream is usually not indicated in the text, and the transformation from reality to the dream state is masked from the reader. This is accomplished either by eliminating from the narrative the moment of lapse into unconsciousness or by inserting a false awakening which is finally revealed as a part of the hero's fantastic dream. The dream sequence itself maintains the temporal synchrony of the narrative. However, this linear movement may be obliterated retrospectively. Within the dream sequence the narrative focus falls upon the protagonist who is experiencing the supernatural phenomenon and expresses his point of view. The final outcome of each story reveals the effect of the transnormal occurrence. The dream may leave the hero in a new and heightened state of perception. Another form of final outcome, however, depicts the protagonist as unchanged but raises the perception of the reader to an awareness of possible retribution for evil.

The supernatural being is most commonly the living corpse of a male or males who are depicted as coming to pay a visit to the living. Grotesque elements predominate in the depiction of these animated corpses. Initial manifestation of the corpse-ghost is visual, followed by subsequent appeals to the auditory and tactile sensory perceptions of the character who experiences the supernatural. Delineation of environmental conditions follows a typical romantic pattern and conditions the occurrence of supernatural phenomena. The psychological state of the protagonist also serves to motivate the manifestation of the supernatural. Frenetic motion, heightened mental states, and excessive imbibing are also linked with the occurrence of transnormal phenomena. Within the dream tale positive Christian supernatural forces do not appear, but their influence is present. The problem of mystery is handled by masking the dream sequence, therein maintaining the ambiguous nature of encounters with the other-worldly. The mystery is further intensified through supernatural shading of the environment and the possible appearance of enigmatic figures subject to both supernatural and rational motivation.

The dream tale then represents an emphatic negation to the question of the true existence of supernatural phenomena because the dream frame is intended to show that allegedly "supernatural" events occur only within the real world. This case against the supernatural was clearly stated by Odoevskiy himself when he wrote:

> It seems to me that beneath all these fantastic tales of frightening events of various types there are concealed a number of natural phenomena up to now not sufficiently studied, and the reasons for which may be found partially within man himself and partially within his environment. . .I wish to explain all of these horrific phenomena and to place them under the general laws of nature, to promulgate the annihilation of superstitious fears.[32]

Odoevskiy and his fellow writers of dream tales provided stories of the otherworldly which serve not only to engage the reader but also to dissuade him from any superstitious belief in the existence of supernatural phenomena.

FOOTNOTES

[1]"Brigadier" first appeared in the anthology Novosel'e, Part I (St. Petersburg, 1833), and was later incorporated by Odoevskiy in the "Fourth Night" of his Russian Nights. The text used for this study was V.F. Odoevskiy, Russkie Nochi (Munich: Slavische Propylaen, 1967), 97-109.

[2]Ibid., p. 97.

[3]Ibid.

[4]Ibid.

[5]Ibid., p. 98.

[6]Ibid., p. 99.

[7]Ibid, p. 108.

[8]Ibid., p. 109.

[9]Also incorporated to form part of the "Fourth Night," "A Corpse's Mockery" was first published in the almanac, Dennitsa na 1834-iy god (Moscow, 1834). The text used for this study was the Slavische Propylaen edition, pp. 117-129.

[10]Ibid., p. 119.

[11]Ibid., p. 123.

[12]Ibid.

[13]Ibid., p. 127.

[14]"The Live Corpse" first appeared in the journal Notes of the Fatherland, XXXIII, 1844. Utilized for this study was the text which appeared in Russkie povesti XIX-veka 20-kh - 30-kh godov, II (Moscow-Leningrad, 1950), 227-248.

[15]"The Terrible Divination" was first published in the journal Moscow Telegraph Nos. 5-6 (1831). The text used in this

study was A.A. Bestuzhev-Marlinskiy. Sochineniya v dvukh tomakh, I (Moscow, 1958), 311-342.

[16]Ibid., p. 316.

[17]Ibid., p. 329.

[18]Ibid., p. 331.

[19]Ibid., p. 341.

[20]"The Undertaker" was first published in 1831 under the title Povesti pokoynogo Ivana Petrovicha Belkina, izdannye A.P. Utilized for this study was the text appearing in A.S. Pushkin, Sochineniya v tryokh tomakh, III (Moscow, 1954), 252-258.

[21]Ibid., p. 252.

[22]Ibid., p. 256.

[23]Ibid.

[24]Ibid., p. 255.

[25]Ibid., p. 256.

[26]Ibid., p. 257.

[27]Ibid., p. 256.

[28]Ibid., p. 257.

[29]M.O. Gershenzon, "Sny Pushkina," Stat'i o Pushkine. Istoriya i teoriya iskusstv, Vypusk I (Moscow, 1926), 96-110.

[30]S. G. Bocharov, "O smysle 'Grobovshchika'," Kontekst-1973. Literaturno - teoreticheskie issledovaniya (Moscow, 1974), 196-230.

[31]B. Eykhenbaum, "Problemy poetiki Pushkina," Skvoz' literaturu (Leningrad, 1924), 167.

[32]This quote occurred in "Pis'ma knyagine E.P.R." in Sochineniya knyazya V.F. Odoevskogo, Part 3 (St. Petersburg, 1844), 308.

CHAPTER THREE

ANECDOTES OF THE OTHERWORLDLY

We have seen that Russian writers of dream tales not only attempted to debunk the supernatural but also manifested an incipient interest in moral problems and human psychology. In addition the Russians proved to be master practitioners of a second type of supernatural tale in which transnormal occurrences are framed as internarrative anecdotes, wherein different narrators speculate about supernatural occurrences which they themselves did not witness. These chains of anecdotes form complete tales and exhibit similar characteristics. Like the dream tale, the supernatural anecdote is subject to humorous as well as serious treatment. This category, however, exhibits the complex problem of motivation for alleged occurrences of the supernatural, an issue not so pertinent to the dream frame which itself serves as the final rationale for all events.

It appears that the internal compositional laws which govern this type of tale require that supernatural anecdotes be aimed at rational motivation as jokes, ruses, spoofs on naive folk, or cases of mistaken identity often involving an ironic test of a non-believer in extrasensory phenomena. Even if final rational motivation for events is not provided within a given story, clues and hints are carefully embedded within the narrative and strongly indicate rational bases for all alleged transnormal phenomena. Typical of this anecdotal type of short story are Somov's "The Monster," Bestuzhev's "Cuirassier" and "An Evening at the Caucasian Waters in 1824," Vel'tman's "Alyonushka," Odoevskiy's "The Apparition," and Gogol''s "Fair at Sorochinsy."

Somov's delightful "The Monster"[1] is the least complex example of this story type and consists of a single anecdote narrated by the peasant Faddey who is entertaining his passenger as the two drive along the open road. Faddey tells of a monster, called "Kikimora," which allegedly has occupied the home of a prosperous peasant, Pankrat Panteleev. Curious happenings in the Panteleev household concern their granddaughter, Varya, whose grandmother would put the child to bed in an unkempt condition, unwashed and uncombed. The young girl, however, would awaken completely groomed, her faced washed and hair combed. The oldsters immediately assume that an impure spirit has settled in their home. Even though the grandparents are unable to discern anything particularly evil in the activities of this rather helpful sprite, as pious folk they do not wish to house an evil spirit. As a result the Panteleevs appeal to their village priest, Father Saveley, to rid them of the monster. The priest, an enlightened individual, attempts to dissuade them from their superstitious beliefs by denying the existence of domestic monsters in general and by assuring the Panteleevs that they have dreamed up the whole affair.

45

There was in the village a mysterious German steward, a teller of supernatural tales, to whom the unhappy family now appeals in their continuing campaign to rid the household of this monster. The enterprising German readily agrees to evict the impure spirit, but his drunken efforts bear no fruit, and the Panteleevs find themselves instead swindled out of one hundred rubles and several bottles of wine.

Meanwhile, the monster begins to engage in every sort of prank and even ceases dressing and grooming tiny Varya. For an entire year the family lives in desperation when one day a poverty-stricken old woman in rags appears at their door. Having enjoyed the full hospitality of the Panteleevs and having heard of the evil spirit which had lodged in their home, the old woman agrees to help. After carrying out a series of complicated instructions provided by the old seeress, including harnessing a horse and cow to a sled (even though it is summer), sweeping the entire house while producing a certain incantation, and throwing three handfuls of earth over the shoulder while spitting, the Panteleevs finally manage to rid themselves of their pesky guest. In addition the old woman succeeds in reviving Varya who is in a deathlike trance, having fallen from the roof of the house at the height of the commotion caused by the monster, and the story ends happily.

With the close of the anecdote the enlightened passenger, representing the authorial point of view, emerges to provide a rational explanation for all events. This gentleman explains that the old women of the village were probably envious of the prosperous Panteleev family and impersonated the monster for lack of any other sort of entertainment. These same old women then spread rumors through the whole village, and the story was passed down from generation to generation. Thus the tale ends with a thorough debunking of the supernatural.

Somov's story exemplifies the treatment of allegedly supernatural phenomena, which was to become characteristic of the anecdote. Initially the narrator, old Faddey, reports that he was but twelve years old when the events occurred. This allows for the blurring of time and indicates that the original occurrences were reported by a child who naively believes in the supernatural. The monster is never seen by anyone and exists only through rapidly spreading and pyramiding rumors.

The Panteleev family decides to stay by Varya's bedside and witness for themselves the strange happenings in the house. This scene depicting their futile attempts is constructed so that the entire family is open to ridicule for their superstitious beliefs:

Not long before the crowing of the first cock
sleep overcame them, and everyone fell asleep
right where he was sitting. It was funny to
look at them. One would be snoring and
pinching his nose between his knees. Another wanted to scratch himself behind the ear
and was swaying so much in his sleep that his
finger would go back and forth through the air
like a pendulum on the big clock in the Master's
house. A third one yawned clear to his ears,
and when sleep overcame him he still hadn't
closed his mouth and was all stiffened up. A
fourth rocked back and fell under a bench and
slept there until he woke up. And all the time
when they were sleeping the grooming of Varya
went on as usual. By morning she was trimmed,
washed, combed, and sleeked up like a little
doll.[2]

Even little Varya is unable to explain what is happening to her,
for she sleeps through the activities of the alleged monster.
Faddey admits that he saw nothing even though he was watching
as the monster was finally driven out into the forest. Faddey
does relate that his aunt Afimya had heard from her neighbor
who heard from still a third party that a certain old woman in
the village had seen the monster in the form of a large grey cat.
It must be noted, however, that even Aunt Afimya's report
comes ten years after the event.

In addition Varya's strange behavior which culminates in
her disastrous plunge from the roof is described from the point
of view of the family members:

Most frightening of all was this. Suddenly they
saw little Varya, who was playing outside, stop
in the middle of the yard and, waving her little
hands, look for a long time at the roof as if
someone were beckoning to her and, without
taking her eyes from the roof, she rushed to
the wall and began to clamber up onto it like
a kitten. She climbed up to the very top of
the roof and stood up, folding her little hands
as if sentenced to death. All the members of
the family raised their arms. Everyone without
even blinking an eye watched as the little girl
raised her eyes toward heaven and stood as if
rooted to the very top, pale as linen and without taking a breath. Judge for yourself, Baron
Sir, what it must have been like for her own

folks to see little Varya suddenly fly headfirst
from the roof as if she'd been shot out of a
cannon.[3]

These impressionable folk may well be attributing supernatural
coloration to this event where there should be none.

Thus reports of the monster are shrouded in rumor and
hearsay, and accounts of the supernatural are removed many
years from the time of the original occurrences. Narrators are
gullible and superstitious peasants who harbor a naive belief in
supernatural phenomena. Somov, while preserving the colorful
dialect of the Russian peasantry and creating characters reminiscent of Russian folklore, nevertheless asserts the necessity that
superstition be overcome through education and rationalism.

"The Cuirassier"[4] is another example of a simply constructed anecdotal type of supernatural tale and consists of a basic
frame story linked with two anecdotes which are provided with
rational resolutions for supernatural encounters. Narrated by a
partisan officer leading Russian troops in pursuit of the French,
the story opens with a battle between the two opposing forces.
A mysterious gigantic warrior enters the Russian ranks and spurs
them on to victory over the enemy. There is nothing unusual in
the narrator's description of this warrior except for his colossal
size. The common soldiers, however, described by the narrator
as "gullible" and "blind," seem to find something supernatural in
the stranger's gigantic form, fearless bearing, and commanding
voice.

This same theme of simple people attributing supernatural
characteristics to natural phenomena is evident in the description
of an approaching French prisoner who is described by one soldier as possessing arms with long claws, with the apocalyptical
number 666 imprinted on his face, and with a belly which wasn't
satisfied even having swallowed up all of Europe.

The initial anecdote is the story of the old Glinskiy manor
where the soldiers find rest for the night. This story of the
supernatural is narrated from the point of view of the castle's
old steward who had heard the tale from a third party no longer
among the living. It seems that Felitsa, the master's daughter,
had been visited regularly by a mysterious horseman who appeared like an apparition without leaving any tracks. It was
reported that the girl had garnered miraculous knowledge from
this ghost. After one visit she claimed to know the very hour
of her death.

The castle servants interpreted this and other mysterious
events as of supernatural origin. Each Friday Felitsa had sat

48

alone, and it seemed to the servants that she was talking with someone whom they never saw. Finally the servants heard a mysterious presence descend the staircase even though the outer doors were locked, all of which they considered some sort of miracle. After this occurrence Felitsa was found lying on the floor in a faint. On the very next night at the first sight of the new moon the unfortunate girl expired. As a result the servants connected the death of their mistress with the position of the moon, which they considered to possess supernatural influence over mortals.

The anecdote now concludes with no apparent rationalization and gives way to a second story which is narrated by a certain Zarnitskiy, a soldier under the command of the frame narrator. This story concerns the narrator's aunt, Liza, and her lover Bayanov. Imprisoned by her father, who had refused permission for her to marry, Liza had died in incarceration. Rumors had circulated that Bayanov had also been thrown into one of the castle cellars and had died there. Stories of moans and groans were circulated by servants who asserted that they recognized the voice of Liza's teacher-lover. Rumors of miracles in the house, of doors which opened by themselves, of steps which rang out when no one was to be seen, and accounts of prolonged moanings are described from the point of view of the servants. These reports and mysterious happenings were so unnerving to Liza's cruel father that he rushed out of his bedroom one night clad only in a nightshirt and ordered a carriage. Having left, he never again returned to the castle and was found dead in bed a year and a half later.

This anecdote is followed by the narrator's comment that simple people, who were certain that they had seen teeth marks on the old count's neck, said that he had been devoured by evil spirits to whom he had sold his soul. Intelligent people, however, said that it was God's justice. Thus dissemination of rumors concerning supernatural occurrences is attributed to ignorant servants, and it is revealed that the narrator was not an eyewitness to the events which he describes. No ghost or shade actually appeared but was invented in answer to various unexplained events which had occurred within the household. This supports the frame narrator's general attitude asserting nonbelief in the supernatural.

The narrator, Zarnitskiy, now relates various childhood experiences which had occurred when together with his mother and brother he had visited that very castle. The boy's mother and various household servants had spent many hours relating to the young brothers various legends concerning the old domicile. Upon one occasion when the narrator's brother was entering the old castle, he came rushing headlong down the steps confessing that the old house had looked terrifyingly at him with a frosty breath, and that door hinges scraped like teeth. This adventure is depicted from the point of view of the brother and underscores his infantile belief in the supernatural.

Zarnitskiy now confesses that at times the boys imagined that the castle was chasing them. The moaning wind and broken windows all seemed to be evidence of spirits with news from the other world. The plasterless walls, revealing grillwork in the construction of the castle, resembled to the child the decaying body of a rich man whose skin and clothing had fallen and bared his ribs. Everything in the room seemed to have supernatural significance. A "monster" which once chased the boys from the castle turned out to be a cat. The scene is described from the point of view of the narrator as a child and supports the assertion that supernatural events occur only to children and simple, naive folk.

The narrator now recalls that as an adult he had visited the old castle once more. At the very moment when thoughts of Liza were passing through his mind, the impressionable officer heard the sound of mysterious footsteps in an adjoining room. Having told that he glanced into the chamber which had served as Liza's cell, Zarnitskiy reports:

> And suddenly, in reality, without any doubt,
> before me there really was. . .[5]

The narrative is now suspended and returns to the present as heavy steps are also heard on the stairs leading into the room where the storytelling is taking place. The frame narrator ironically confesses that at that moment both he and Zarnitskiy were so inclined toward a belief in the supernatural that they turned their eyes to the door with a certain timid expectation. The resounding footsteps belong to the mysterious warrior who had appeared in battle that very day and had led the Russian troops to victory. Supernatural coloration is present in references to the warrior's ghostly appearance. These comments, however, are constructed from the point of view of the young soldiers who are depicted as uneducated and foolish.

The cuirassier is in a state of frenzy and, believing that he sees Liza's ghost, confesses his love and promises to avenge her murder. The rather elusive spook, however, is not manifest to any of the others assembled in the room. The delirious warrior is carried into an adjoining room where he is left to rest, and the conversants return to hear the conclusion of Zarnitskiy's anecdote which had been interrupted at the point where he opened the door of the old dungeon in which Liza had been imprisoned. Zarnitskiy reports that he encountered an apparition which appeared to be a woman all in white. This ghost is manifest only visually, and the moment of encounter is rendered solely from the point of view of the astonished Russian:

> I took a look. In this room a candle was burn-
> ing. Under a window covered with grillwork
> there was a table. In the corner stood a simple
> bed and on it--imagine my surprise!--there was
> a woman in a white dress--who in the world
> was it? Liza![6]

The narrator's ensuing ironic remark, in which he states the conviction that so much life could not possibly be focused in a corpse, foreshadows a natural rationalization for the appearance of this ethereal being. After admonishing the frame narrator to guess the identity of the apparition, Zarnitskiy explains that the "ghost" was really his aunt, the daughter of Liza and Bayanov. Thus the mysterious apparition is revealed to be a mortal, just as the reader suspects.

The cuirassier now concludes the tale by revealing that he is Felitsa's lost lover, the "otherworldly" visitor who had always called on Fridays. This motivates the warrior's strange behavior on the preceding day and provides rational causation for the servants' tales. The cuirassier, however, remains adamant that the ghost of Felitsa had indeed appeared to him on the previous evening. The frame narrator and Zarnitskiy attempt to dissuade him with the rational explanation that he had seen Felitsa's portrait, which had engendered a hallucinatory dream. The cuirassier is firm in his belief that the apparition has heralded his impending demise. The exact nature of this episode remains unresolved, and the tale concludes with the ironic death of the cuirassier as he had formerly predicted. Even though final rational motivation for this episode is not provided, the reader is inclined to accept the narrator's theory that Felitsa's ghost was the product of the frustrated warrior's enflamed imagination.

"The Cuirassier" further establishes a typical pattern for tales of its type. The main narrative is punctuated by anecdotes detailing alleged supernatural phenomena which are provided with rational resolutions in turn removed from the basic exposition of events. Distancing is accomplished by narrative interruptions which link each anecdote with the main narrative. The atmosphere of mystery is further intensified through presentation of ironic and unresolved events such as the apparent foreknowledge of death on the part of poor Felitsa and her warrior-lover. However, even these unexplained phenomena are extenuated by hints which would negate possible supernatural motivation for events.

Anecdotes of the supernatural represent a synthesis of many different points of view (soldiers, the castle orderly and other servants, as well as children). The tendency is for supernatural events to be recounted by a narrator who was not himself a recent eyewitness to events described. Those witnessing the events later revealed as hearsay are always the uneducated and naive such as young soldiers or peasants. The narrator who himself experienced the supernatural is depicted as a child or one under the influence of a frenetic emotional state. These viewpoints are in fact subordinate to and support the basic authorial contention that the supernatural does not exist, that alleged transnormal events are always rationally motivated. This overall didactic assertion is expressed in digressions which underscore rational causation for alleged supernatural events, and in an ironic narrative tone which exposes believers in supernatural phenomena as uneducated, unenlightened, and foolish. Representing the authorial viewpoint, Zarnitskiy's comments on the origin of belief in the supernatural clearly illustrate this position:

> You ask where did this spring of delights
> burst through from, this relocation of dreamy
> phantoms into real life and of real things into
> sleepy dreams? It seems to me that respon-
> sible for this was the early belief in appari-
> tions, goblins, house-spirits, and in all the
> citizens of the republic beyond the grave, in
> all of the snowy sons of the imagination of
> mothers and nannies, lovers of superstitions;
> and just as responsible were the early doubts
> about all of this. Nanny told me frightening
> things with such simple-heartedness, with
> such inner conviction. My parents and
> teachers in turn talked about them with such
> contempt and self-assurance that I contin-
> ually vacillated between reason and prej-
> udice, between the deceptive charm of the
> miraculous and the strict proof of truth.
> Which was to emerge victorious, the side
> of impression or of conviction? It isn't dif-
> ficult to guess. To tell the truth, man al-
> ways prefers that which he isn't able to com-
> prehend to that which he has no inclination
> to comprehend.[7]

A structurally more complex tale formed by a rather lengthy chain of anecdotes is "An Evening at the Caucasian Waters in 1824,"[8] which consists of a series of five interwoven stories. The frame narrator is himself a gentleman traveling through the Caucasus Mountains, one of ten romantics who swap yarns after dinner at an inn. The anecdotal repartee is prefaced by the frame narrator's remark that the Caucasian waters had a certain magic property for the assembled company. Because the discussion is preceded by much toasting and clicking of glasses in a bacchanalian atmosphere, the stories of supernatural events are often linked readily with imbibing.

The initial anecdote, a tale concerning the robbery of Grecian merchants from Byzantium, including many references to magic and buried treasure, reverts to prehistory and is unverifiable. The second tale, the story of the mysterious death of a certain Hungarian, is narrated by one of the assembled gentlemen, who wears a green frock coat. This gentleman's tale was supposedly related to him by a friend who had lived next door to the Hungarian and who overheard but was not a witness to the events which he describes.

The scene of the Hungarian's death and the mysterious presence of an extraterrestrial voice is described by the man in the green coat who reports that his friend had heard two series of footsteps and a ghostly voice in the Hungarian's room following his death. The narrator is in the process of describing how the doors to the Hungarian's apartment were thrown open when the action suddenly returns to the Caucasian inn and is suspended with the words:

And he saw...[9]

The tale now returns to the frame situation in which the doors to the hall open with a crash, and the reactions of the various participants in the discussion are catalogued. All of these "enlightened" gentlemen obviously believe in the supernatural, for they appear to be horrified at the report of this encounter with the otherworldly. The main narrative now focuses upon these listeners who momentarily become the object of investigation instead of serving as the source of the narration. This altered narrative focus becomes external and emphasizes the appearance, actions, and statements of the assembled gentlemen. Typical, for instance, is the statement:

Judging by his face and actions...[10]

By suspending the narrative the author is able to ridicule the assembled company who are gently chided for their superstitious beliefs.

One of the listeners is a retired colonel, and the reader now discovers that it was his nephew, a friend of the deceased Hungarian, who had come bursting into the room much to the horror of those gathered there. A strange imprint on the nephew's jacket remains unexplained, and the man in the green frock coat reports that coincidentally it was exactly a year ago to the very hour when the Hungarian passed away so mysteriously. The young nephew's strange behavior and sudden exit from the room followed by his uncle also remain an enigma. As a result of these recondite actions the mystery is intensified but remains unsolved, and another storyteller emerges.

The third anecdote, a story which allegedly occurred five years before the time of the frame story, is narrated by a new storyteller, a dragoon captain, and concerns the fantastic adventures of his brother who was a sailor. The narrator relates that his brother's encounter with the supernatural was preceded by much drinking and merrymaking. Soon there developed a discussion concerning the plausibility of the existence of the supernatural, and the brother who was a doubter boastfully dared his friends to test his courage. It was then decided that the seaman would approach a hanging corpse and invite it to dinner at the very inn where the sailors were assembled. In order to verify his act the young man was ordered to tie a golden shoelace around the corpse's left arm.

The sailor makes his way toward the fatal assignation in an atmosphere of sinister foreboding. The surroundings are bathed in eerie moonlight with windmills standing out like ghosts and giants. Initial perception of the animated corpse is tactile and is described from the point of view of the surprised sailor:

> At the very instant when his fingers embraced
> the leaden hand of the hanging man the city
> clock began to strike midnight, and its plain-
> tive boom carried by the wind seemed to the
> brother more sad than a funeral knell. To-
> gether with and in addition to this he felt
> the corpse press his hand and shake it in
> a friendly fashion.[11]

The narrator now reveals that his brother's head was swimming from overimbibing. Thus the reader falsely suspects that the live corpse is probably the result of a drunken hallucination.

Immediate visual perception of the corpse shaking and rattling its members now follows. The brother perceives the indistinct voice of the corpse emanating from various positions in the vicinity. At this instant the narrative is again interrupted, and members of the original group speculate upon this disembodied voice. It is suggested that the corpse may be a ventriloquist reminiscent of the corpse-oracles from antiquity. The enigma, however, remains unsolved, and the narrative continues.

The corpse's instructions to the baffled sailor now follow, whereupon the gullible mortal agrees to dig for buried treasure

54

at a certain spot and entrust it to the hanged criminal's innocent victim. The two then shake hands in agreement:

> He extended his hand to the dead man. 'I'm
> grateful', said the latter pressing the brother's
> hand, and at that moment it didn't seem so cold
> to him as before.[12]

The reader now suspects that the "corpse" may really be a mortal involved in playing a joke upon the unsuspecting and naive sailor.

An additional indication that the sailor may be the victim of a hoax surfaces in the digging scene. While engaged in unearthing the "treasure," the sailor hears whistles, hands clapping, leaves falling from a tree above, and stones pelting about him. Finally he strikes something hard, and at that instant a heavy object knocks the unfortunate young man senseless into the very hole which he had been digging. Thus an encounter with the supernatural has led into a lapse of consciousness which reinforces the reader's false conclusion that the entire episode is a hallucination.

While lying in a semiconscious state, the sailor hears the neighing of horses, the knock of wheels and the chatter of people. In twenty-four hours he regains consciousness back in the tavern where the wager was originally consumated. The reader may now theorize that the partially conscious sailor was transported to the inn by his friends who had perpetrated the joke. The whole episode could not have been a dream because the sailor finds a one-hundred-pound note along with a letter signed by his friends, in which they acknowledge that he has won the bet and proved his courage. The mystery remains officially unsolved. However, the evidence overwhelmingly justifies the joke theory of motivation for alleged "supernatural" events.

The moral element enters this anecdote at the point where the sailor stands before the gallows upon which the hanging corpse is suspended. The narrator surveys the place of execution and comments:

> It is unpleasant not only at night but also dur-
> ing the day to see the detestable picture of
> moral and physical destruction presented to us
> by capital punishment.[13]

Thus the sailor's fantastic adventure is linked with the presentation of a moral lesson, an attack upon the legal institution of capital punishment.

At the close of this anecdote various speculations are proffered by the assembled gentlemen who debate the cause for events. A dream is one of the suggested motivations as is the supposition that it was all a joke. The narrator, however, rejects these speculations:

> My brother didn't tell me anything like that,
> and I don't think that you have any reason
> to doubt my words.[14]

The supernatural encounter remains officially unexplained, but the joke motivation is certainly most plausible.

The next anecdote is presented by an artillery officer and concerns the adventures of his uncle in Poland during the Polish civil war. Accompanying the uncle is his orderly, Zarubaev, who believes in evil spirits, Kievan witches, and who often makes the sign of the Cross. Having come upon an old Polish castle, they are entertained for the night by the Poles who live there. The uncle drinks much at the supper table, and their Polish host spins a yarn concerning the history of the old castle, a tale of the Polish Count Glemba who had murdered his lover, Bianca Menottie, by pouring boiling lead into her ear. Tormented by his conscience, Glemba dreamed every night that he saw apparitions. All of the house servants also were convinced that they had seen a woman in white with long flowing hair. This female ghost had supposedly run all over the castle, and having met the count, had threatened him with her finger pointing to heaven, and then had disappeared.

More toasting follows the story of Count Glemba, and the uncle falls into a deep sleep only to awaken at midnight and contemplate all that had happened during the evening. The nocturnal stillness, full moon, and chilly wind lead the partially inebriated Russian to thoughts of corpses, water nymphs, and house spirits. Portraits on the walls seem about to jump from their frames in an attempt to annihilate the uninvited guest.

Unable to sleep any longer, the uncle now wanders about the castle in an attempt to locate his friend Zarubaev. Much to his horror the somewhat confused Russian discovers his friend on the verge of death lying in a pool of blood. With his last breath Zarubaev describes the appearance of a phantom in white, pale as death, which had appeared and chased away the Poles as they were about to kill the unsuspecting Russians.

The uncle once more proceeds down the corridor and up two staircases where he finds an empty room, but is still unable to sleep because of the haunting memories of the corpse of Zarubaev and the apparition. The furnishings of this place are cast in supernatural hues. The room, which is adorned with fantastic animal heads, becomes sinister and eerie in the reflected moonlight. The sudden appearance of a female apparition is depicted from the uncle's point of view:

> My uncle again glanced at her, and his hair
> stood on end; frost penetrated to the very
> heart of his bones--It was a woman corpse!![15]

The incredulous Russian first perceives the sound of the ghost's light footsteps on the floorboards. He then feels her hot breath on his cheek, and finally sees the corpse-apparition. A fourth area of perception is now added as the Russian asserts that this female apparition smells like the grave. The uncle describes the corpse as pale, with bloodless veins and pupilless eyes. Even though the agitated Russian perceives this creature as a ghost, the reader suspects from the creature's hot breath and other human attributes that the "ghost" is really a mortal in disguise.

The phantom approaches, and the uncle fears that she will begin to gnaw at him, but the ghost remains satisfied with a kiss and motions that he should follow. Having led him back safely to the Russian lines, the apparition reveals that she is in reality the wife of a Polish Russian who had settled in the castle. Intending to frighten away the Poles, she had donned a white dress and had applied white make-up in order to appear to be a spook. The supernatural event is now resolved with completely realistic motivation, and the anecdote comes to a close.

Comprising the fifth anecdote is a Hussar officer's tale of an adventure which he experienced three years previous to the time of the narration. Lost in bad weather, he had come upon a chapel and had discovered inside a corpse covered with a shroud. The Russian believed that he perceived an odor of death emanating from the corpse, but soon realized that this smell was simply meat cooking near the body. In the flickering light of the icon lamp it seems to the narrator that the corpse raises its head slightly. This occurrence is described from his own point of view:

> I took a half-eyed glance at the coffin, and
> it seemed to me that the dead man raised
> his head.[16]

The narrative is now interrupted, and a typical discussion of supernatural phenomena ensues. The narrator, who does not believe in the supernatural, presents a comic analogy between ghosts popping up in the darkness and worms appearing in limburger cheese. He also chides persons who would threaten to catch the Devil by the tail during the daytime but at night would go to great lengths to avoid passing through a cemetery.

A swift return to the anecdote follows with the narrator's description of being awakened by his growling dog which has attacked the "corpse," by now stealthily approaching the unsuspecting Russian with flashing eyes and knife in hand. A battle between the Russian, the "corpse" and his comrades now ensues. The Russian manages to escape from the chapel and leaves the "ghost" bleeding and moaning in pain. In an attempt to escape, the Russian now enters another hut, glimpses yet another corpse, and crumples onto the floor in a faint.

The supernatural encounter at last receives realistic motivation. The soldier's wounded poodle attests to the fact that this experience was not a hallucination caused by the fever which had overtaken him. The second peasant hut, which he had found at random in the dark, was the home of a peasant whose mother had died recently, and the terrified Russian had interrupted her funeral service. A search party sent to the original chapel uncovered remnants left by the robbers. Unnerved by his experience, the narrator reports that he was senseless for six weeks after the terrible encounter, another lapse into unconsciousness following an alleged encounter with the supernatural.

The story of the colonel's nephew and the mysterious Hungarian remains unresolved. The narrator, however, remarks that he is personally acquainted with the colonel who will be able to explain everything. The reader assumes that a natural explanation for the mystery may be forthcoming. Thus the chain of anecdotes comes to a close with all supernatural occurrences receiving actual motivation or alleged explanation from within the real world.

Bestuzhev's story is typical of the anecdotal type of supernatural tale in which otherworldly encounters are subject to rational motivation even if such justification is not presented openly within the story. Rationalization need not necessarily follow the description of the supernatural encounter but may be placed after a subsequent anecdote, or definite rational resolution may be totally absent. If this is the case, strong hints are present within the story and indicate decisively the possibility of a natural explanation for alleged supernatural phenomena. Unexplained phenomena may be removed far into the past and relegated to the form of rumor or hearsay, as is the case with the tale of the robbery of the Byzantine merchants.

Supernatural events receive environmental coloration which exacerbates the mystery and lends credence to alleged phenomena which are subsequently to be rationalized naturally. Occurrences of the supernatural are usually nocturnal and are linked with cemeteries, coffins, or other symbols of death. The supernatural being itself is most commonly an animated corpse which is manifest audibly, visibly, tangibly and even olfactorily. Encounters with the supernatural are experienced by those afflicted with frenetic emotional states or with imaginations heightened through overimbibing, and an encounter with the supernatural is usually followed by a lapse into unconsciousness. This suggests the possibility that supernatural encounters may be the result of hallucinations. In addition, depiction of supernatural phenomena is often linked with the didactic. For example, the scene involving the animated corpse hanging on the gallows serves as a vehicle for the author's attack upon capital punishment, and the tale of Polish Count Glemba promotes the concept of retribution for evil.

The element of mystery is extenuated through supernatural shading of the environment, through unexplained and mysterious events, and resolutions which are removed from the original anecdotal exposition. Supernatural elements are so structured that the narrative may be interrupted or suspended. An interrupted narrative allows for speculation upon the veracity of supernatural phenomena in general. A suspended narrative redirects the narrative focus which falls upon the discussants themselves who are exposed as superstitious folk unwittingly believing in supernatural phenomena. These characters are duped by what they suppose to be actual occurrences of the supernatural. An ironic narrative tone further debunks belief in the supernatural and serves to negate the saccharine and sentimental romanticism of the Zhukovskiy school.[17] The entire narrative is, in fact, presented from an assertive authorial point of view that supernatural phenomena do not really exist.

Vel'tman's "Alyonushka,"[18] a tale which contains perhaps the most lengthy catalogue of the supernatural in all of Russian literature, serves also as an example of the anecdotal construction of supernatural elements. The initial segment of this story illuminates the growth and development of the hero, Severin. A second section details Severin's love for the heroine, Elena, the daughter of his late father's friend, Ksaveriy Astaf'evich. A third segment of the tale is comprised of events occurring on the evening of the lovers' betrothal. The supernatural is introduced here in the form of anecdotes spun by several old friends who have gathered at the home of Ksaveriy Astaf'evich. These stories of encounters with the otherworld lead into a test of Severin, who claims nonbelief in the irrational. There follows the sudden and mysterious disappearance of Elena, and the conclusion of the story locates Severin after two years of a vain search for his lost love.

The initial structural segment of this tale not only details the psychological development of the hero but also presents the opportunity for an assertion of the rationality of all phenomena. For instance, Pyotr Il'ich, Severin's father, comments:

> For every subject and event there is an ex-
> planation; it's not necessary to beat your
> head against the wall.[19]

The frame narrator in describing Severin's naive and ardent love for Elena reports:

> Inexperience believes everything.[20]

Thus the philosophical grounding upon which the tale is constructed is evident from the onset; namely that all events possess rational cause, and belief in the irrational is the product of inexperience and naivete.

On the evening of his daughter's betrothal Ksaveriy Astaf'evich entertains in honor of his future son-in-law, Severin. Parlor conversation turns to the supernatural when the host reports that he is suffering from a terrible toothache, and the assembled guests suggest various methods of healing, including sympathetic magic. The anecdotal repartee is continued by one of the guests who relates the story of his wife who was allegedly cured of a toothache by wrapping the affected area with a kerchief which had been charmed by a fortune teller. This narrator is termed a scraggy old man, a description which exposes him as a gullible oldster susceptible to belief in the supernatural. The miraculous cure is described from his point of view as a witness but not as a direct participant.

The old gentleman's claims to belief in sympathetic magic lead Severin to disavow all such phenomena. It is Severin's contention that miracles did occur in ancient times but have since ceased because of a lack of substantial belief in their occurrence. The narrator supports this conclusion by stating that it is indeed belief which is most important of all, and he concludes that young people do not believe in sympathetic magic. Severin interjects that he believes neither in sorcery, nor in the whisperings of women, nor in dreams. These claims, of course, elicit discussion concerning the veracity of the supernatural.

The construction of this supernatural element is typical of many others within this story type. The anecdote itself is related by an ignorant member of the older generation given to superstitious belief in the supernatural. In addition, this individual did not himself experience the events described. Severin, a member of the younger and allegedly better educated generation

60

negates the narrator's suggestions. If this anecdote is to follow the pattern of others previously discussed, Severin must soon be subjected to a test of this disbelief and be rebuffed for his doubt.

A second anecdote, narrated by one described only as a "fat man," concerns the ancient Pliny-the-Younger's claim that there resided in his house a spirit who came each night in order to shave the beard of his master. The portly narrator also relates the story of the Greek philosopher Eucrates who saw a citizen of Memphis, Pancrates, jump into the Nile fully clothed. After resting on the river bottom, Pancrates would emerge from the water totally dry and would return to the ship riding on the back of a crocodile.

This yarn is interrupted by one of the listeners who reports that it is indeed possible to remain under the water because he had seen a sorcerer-miller who possessed this rather unusual talent. As a child the narrator had been taken to a distillery by his father. Here the young boy saw a miller who would take a pillow, jump into a whirlpool and sleep several hours only to emerge completely dry, as if he had never been in the water. When this miller put the mill into motion, the wheels and millstones would dance, and the gears would click in rhythm. The boy was afraid to enter the storehouse lest he be eaten by mice.

The original narrator now returns to his tale of Pancrates and Eucrates. Pancrates supposedly amazed Eucrates by dressing and animating an umbrella or broom which he would force to become his personal servant. When the servant was no longer needed, Pancrates would transform him into his former state. Eucrates himself wished to know the secret of how this was accomplished, and having overheard the incantation which brought about the miraculous transformation, he successfully converted a broom to serve in this capacity. However, much to his dismay, Eucrates was unable to stop the transformed water carrier until his house was nearly flooded. The agitated Greek hastened to slash the broom to pieces, but each of the remaining scraps of wood would don a dress in the form of a piece of cloth and would begin carrying still more water. Finally Pancrates returned, discovered what was occurring, and managed to halt the entire process.

These two anecdotes are interwoven. The tales of Pliny-the-Younger and of Pancrates and Eucrates are removed into prehistory and form hearsay not subject to verification. Narrative interruption of the story of Pancrates extenuates the mysterious nature of events and stimulates the reader's interest. The tale of Pancrates is related by another ancient narrator and forms a narration within a narration which is subject to the blurring of time. The anecdote of the sorcerer-miller is rendered from the point of view of the narrator as a child and may be interpreted as the product of childish fantasy not subject to verification. Severin's immediately ensuing remark provides rational motivation for the ancient stories as fables from the works of Goethe.

A fourth anecdote is rendered by another unspecified member of the assembled listeners and concerns the experience of his grandfather who was an orderly to Peter the Great. Having accompanied the Tsar to the home of the famous sorcerer, Bruce, the orderly remained outside and eavesdropped on the interchange between the magician and the Tsar. The grandfather, it seems, overheard the Tsar ordering Bruce to command his sandman to brew coffee. The scene of this eavesdropping is depicted from the point of view of the grandfather. Having heard the Tsar's compliment in regard to the quality of the coffee, the eavesdropper jumped away from the door and could hear nothing more. The anecdote remains mysterious, unrationalized, and is narrated by a character who was not a direct participant in the events which he describes. This curious tale also occasions speculation concerning the true nature of this event. Severin's retort that he believes in the existence of the orderly but not in supernatural animation indicates his continuing skepticism and foreshadows the test of his unbelief, which he is soon to undergo.

The fifth anecdote is narrated by Ksaveriy Astaf'evich and concerns his brother-in-law's encounter with a supernatural evil power. The brother-in-law, having taken possession of a new estate, had ordered that a forest be cut down. This request was promptly refused by the local villagers who claimed that the field belonged to a red stone idol which stood on a high hill overlooking the forest. The villagers insisted that it was necessary to pay the idol tribute. The brother-in-law of course scoffed at this demand and ordered them to cease payment. This negation of the supernatural was soon to be put to the test. The villagers soon claimed that it was impossible for them to cut down the forest because their axes had become dull and their arms refused to swing. The brother-in-law then claimed that he himself would go and cut the forest. Having ordered the horses harnessed, he discovered that the steeds would not allow themselves to be caught. On that day during the late hours the perplexed Russian perceived a shuffling noise in his bedroom. Suddenly something resembling a huge stone fell and pinned him to the floor with all its weight. Having fallen into unconsciousness, the hapless victim was heard to cry out:

> There it is, the red stone gentleman! Oh,
> pray to him so he won't burn me! Tell him
> that I'll give him a tenth of everything![21]

Later, having recovered his health, the Russian left never to re-turn.

Ksaveriy Astaf'evich claims that he himself was a witness to this occurrence. However, the story was related to him by his brother-in-law two years after the actual event. Once again the typical anecdotal pattern of construction is evident. The story is removed temporally from the actual event, and the narrator was not himself an eyewitness. Belief in the animation of the red stone idol is held by the ignorant villagers who claim to have been thwarted by supernatural means in their attempt to cut down the forest. In fact, the very existence of the idol is es-tablished only by rumor and hearsay:

> People say that there is a red stone idol
> standing on a high hill.[22]

An individual who scoffs at the otherworldly is himself put to the test and ironically experiences the supernatural. The brother-in-law's unfortunate encounter occurs at night, and he is depicted as frightened by the huge chambers of the manor house. Barking dogs further frighten the agitated Russian and prepare him for an encounter with the unknown. In order to overcome these fears he attempts to sleep. Thus an encounter with the supernatural is preceded by the victim's emotional arous-al and is also conditioned by temporal factors since the alleged visitation occurs at midnight.

The approach of the stone idol is perceived by the victim initially only audibly and is rendered from his point of view:

> Suddenly, around midnight, he heard some-
> one walking around in the room, just like a
> huge stone. . .moving from place to place.[23]

The occurrence is also perceived by the victim tangibly since the brother-in-law feels the floor shake, but there is no visual per-ception of the supernatural monster. This absence of visual per-ception provides further blurring of the entire incident. There are no eyewitnesses, and an independent narrator is not present. Since the victim of the alleged supernatural visitation is first aroused into a frenetic emotional state followed by a lapse into unconsciousness, the entire episode may be motivated as a hallu-cinatory dream. The story of this encounter is followed by Severin's skeptical remark that the larger part of the described phenomena was probably the result of a feverish delirium. This of course serves to debunk the supernatural, but Severin too is about to face a meeting with representatives from the other world.

Severin's ensuing remark that he does believe in the sympathetic attraction of souls conditions the sixth and final anecdote, Ksaveriy Astaf'evich's tale of the appearance of his wife's ghost. Attempts to dissuade the old man are rejected by his assertion that the gardener had twice seen a woman in a shroud who came into the house at midnight. The doors were locked from the inside, and the dog was about to rush angrily at the phantom, but it merely whined with delight. Ksaveriy continues with the story that he had just fallen asleep when his wife appeared to him and asked where his gold snuffbox was located. While searching under his pillow for the box, Ksaveriy noted that the phantom had disappeared. He was overcome with horror and remained unable to close his eyes until morning.

Once more the subject of a supernatural experience is placed initially into the sleep state which motivates the episode as the result of a dream conditioned by the gardener's tale that he had seen his mistress' ghost. Manifestation of the shrouded phantom is constructed from the point of view of the old man and is perceived by him both visually and audibly. The disappearance of the ghost is also related from Ksaveriy Astaf'evich's point of view with the statement:

Look, she has disappeared![24]

Ksaveriy Astaf'evich's assertion that his wife had vowed to appear to him after death presents the underlying psychological suggestion for motivation of the phenomenon as a dream.

Ksaveriy Astaf'evich's tale of the ghost now serves to link the preceding anecdotes with the main narrative. Severin states that it is the custom with apparitions to appear three times, and he decides to spend the night in the garden and see this phantom for himself. Severin's statement:

The living are more frightening than the dead. . .[25]

indicates his continuing doubt and intention to test Ksaveriy Astaf'evich's claim. Ksaveriy's remark that if Elena knew about this intention she could convince Severin of the existence of ghosts with a single tender look indicates that Elena does not know what Severin intends to do and serves to motivate the "supernatural" occurrence which is shortly to follow. Further motivation is provided in Elena's touching farewell to her father, a scene which occurs just before midnight. Ksaveriy's statement that Elena seems somehow unwell and Severin's remark that she has seemed ill for three days cast suspicion upon the young girl's activities.

Severin now conceals himself in a bush beside the porch and awaits the appearance of the alleged ghostly visitor. The immediate appearance of a ghost is conditioned by the mention of dark moonlight rolling from behind the clouds, rustling leaves, and a strange howling sound in the distance. Initial perception of the appearance of the ghost is constructed from Severin's point of view with the statement:

It seemed to him. . .[26]

The frame narrator, however, serves as an eyewitness and supports the contention that something unusual is occurring by reporting the sound of a key turning in a lock. This, of course, supports a rational explanation for the episode. Rational cause for events is further supported by the statement that the mysterious shade was:

Something resembling a ghost...a ghost that had not outlived its time on earth.[27]

A further indication of the true nature of this phenomenon is provided by the narrator who says:

It wasn't a dead person.[28]

Severin now perceives yet another "apparition" in the shadows. This second ghost pronounces the name, "Elena," as the two merge into one and vanish. It now becomes clear to the reader that the "apparition" is Elena fleeing the household. Severin, who has not espoused a belief in supernatural phenomena, has been put to the test and ironically now emerges as a believer. The narrator's statement that Severin remains on the spot until morning bereft of thought and memory once more links the victim of a supernatural encounter with a lapse into unconsciousness.

The following morning Severin confesses his vision to Ksaveriy Astaf'evich who admits incredulously that it was all a joke and asserts that Severin saw and heard things because of his own fear. Consequently, in an ironic reversal Severin now believes in the supernatural, and Ksaveriy Astaf'evich asserts the rational basis for events as a ruse. It is shortly revealed, however, that Elena has disappeared, and the scene concludes with Severin's exit in a despondent mood. In the final outcome of the tale Severin is seen two years later still engaged in a vain search for his beloved Elena. During a military campaign he encounters an eighteen-year-old girl singing for her supper in a tavern. Severin is struck by the resemblance between this girl, Alyonushka, and his lost love, Elena. For an instant he believes that this young lady is his sweetheart but, having observed her closely, Severin ascertains that she is not Elena, and the story concludes on this twist of fate. Thus Severin's belief in the supernatural has been put to a final test with tragic and inconclusive results.

"Alyonushka" is yet another tale in which all allegedly supernatural events are provided with eventual rational motivation. This natural motivation may be present within the narrative itself or may reside in hints or clues provided by the frame narrator. Most supernatural encounters are narrated by uneducated, superstitious folk or children who commonly espouse an ignorant belief in the supernatural. Narrators who report contacts with the otherworldly are not usually themselves the victims of the encounter. Exceptions include the tale related by a child whose puerile imagination motivates events, and the story in which the ghost appears to Ksaveriy Astaf'evich, which is motivated both as a dream and a joke played upon the unsuspecting hero. Severin's encounter with the otherworldly is constructed in such a way that the reader readily identifies the "ghost" as his sweetheart participating in an assignation with another. Nonmotivated supernatural events are removed into prehistory and are explained away as legends or fairy tales.

Events within the frame narrative are interwoven with the continuous string of supernatural anecdotes. Because of this the purposefully mysterious and ambiguous nature of events is strengthened, and the reader's interest is heightened. Supernatural encounters themselves are conditioned by environmental factors and lead the victim of alleged supernatural phenomena into a state of unconsciousness. Visual perception of allegedly otherworldly visitations is often blurred with resulting perception of supernatural encounters often rendered through other sensory areas. The supernatural power itself may not be definitively manifest but may exist only according to rumor. Contacts with the otherworldly are detailed from the point of view of the victim. However, an eyewitness narrator may emerge only to support a rational explanation for events. In the final analysis construction of all supernatural elements is subject to the authorial frame narrator's presupposition that the supernatural does not exist, and that reality itself forms the basis for all alleged supernatural encounters.

Odoevskiy's "The Apparition,"[29] another story of the anecdotal type, serves as a microcosm of this category in which various literary devices are exaggerated and parodied. This delightful spoof presents four traveling companions who exchange ideas on the supernatural and spin yarns in order to pass the time.

66

The first anecdote, occasioned as the travellers pass an old castle, is narrated by Iriney Modestovich, a perky little fellow who walks with a hop. Iriney describes the home of his neighbor, Mar'ya Sergeevna. His remark:

In my youth[30]

betrays that what Iriney is about to relate occurred some years before and allows for the typical blurring of time. Iriney's description of his hostess' charming personality is interrupted by his traveling companions who discuss at length the conventions of behavior at social gatherings. This, of course, delays the anecdote itself, and the mystery is humorously heightened. This conversational repartee parodies typical narrative interruptions so characteristic of this particular type of supernatural tale. Iriney Modestovich's remarks on the subject of ghosts present the basic tone of the narrative and exemplify the author's essential message that the supernatural is always subject to rational explanation and simply does not exist:

> These subjects usually catch general attention; our minds, exhausted by the prose of life, are unwillingly attracted by these mysterious occurrences which comprise the current poetry of our society and serve as proof that from poetry as from original sin, no one may escape in this life.[31]

Iriney Modestovich now continues his tale, and the scene forms a charming parody on supernatural encounters which test an individual who claims disbelief in the otherworldly. According to Iriney his story occurred in the depths of autumn with its drenching rains and flooding waters, weather conditions appropriate for discussions of transnormal occurrences. Four guests had appeared in their charming hostess' living room awaiting their partners for a round of cards. However, because of the weather the other guests failed to appear, and those present turned to chatting about many things, including the supernatural. One of the assembled gentlemen did not believe in such phenomena and scofffed at stories of people materializing after death, faces appearing in a third-story window, and dancing tables.

This nonbeliever now relates a tale which forms an anecdote within the original anecdote, and is the story of his father who once saw an apparition with a pale countenance and melancholy expression. The narrator's father had simply stuck out his tongue at the phantom, which was so surprised that it never dared to appear again. Of course, since the narrator's father is now dead, he is unable to verify this rather unusual account,

67

and the narrator himself was not present during the miraculous occurrence. Nevertheless, the narrator assures the assembled company that he follows his father's method, especially when encountering romantic tales in popular journals. Even though a confirmed nonbeliever in the supernatural, this gentleman offers to relate a story so horrific as to guarantee that the listener's hair will literally stand on end.

The events of this tale, allegedly having occurred thirty years previous to Iriney Modestovich's story, now form yet another anecdote within an anecdote. The narrator reports that at that time he was a young soldier quartered in the home of a prosperous landowner, a very fine woman. Nearby on a low hill there stood an ancient castle which often aroused the curiosity of guests gathered at the woman's house. In an aside the narrator remarks that due to a lowering in standards of good taste such castles were then in style, and the soldiers made fun of such ancient architecture. Thus the romantic era with its haunted castles and supernatural encounters becomes the subject of ridicule and satirical comment.

When quizzed about the old castle, the hostess replies with the story of Countess N. This tale now becomes a story within a story within still another story and forms a convincing and humorous parody on the anecdotal construction of supernatural encounters. The ensuing story is of a young countess, cursed by her mother because she had eloped, and finally reconciled after the birth of a child. The old countess, fearing the evil influence of the curse, committed her renunciation to a scrap of paper and placed it in a medallion which she forced her daughter to wear at all times.

Many years pass and the story is related once again from the point of view of the soldier-narrator who tells of the cordial reception he and his friends received at the home of the "young" countess. During a lengthy and most pleasant visit the soldiers have the opportunity to meet the young countess' son, a soldier who has returned home on leave. The young man is quartered in a certain bedroom which had gained the reputation of frightening its occupants with strange sounds and visions. The young man, however, claims disbelief in the supernatural and, of course, must be put to the test for his doubt. On the evening of the guests' departure a grand ball is staged for their benefit. The soldiers dance almost until dawn, but the countess' young son tires early and withdraws to his sleeping quarters. In a fit of pique the countess suggests that he be taught a lesson for leaving the dance floor with so many pretty ladies unattended. Dressed as apparitions the countess and her fellow pranksters approach the son's bedroom. This scene depicting the approach of a row of white apparitions is described from the startled young man's point of view with the statement:

He saw. . .[32]

Initial perception of this phenomenon, however, is audial since the squeak of the door awakens the young soldier. This is also an indication that the apparitions may be mortals who are forced to use the door for their entrance. Typical of all supernatural anecdotes, the episode is linked with the dream state and with an environment cast in strange hues by a pale light. The joke, however, is ironically reversed as the frightened young soldier fires a shot into the crowd of ghosts.

The countess' cry that she had forgotten to put on her mother's medallion explains the presence of the "phantoms" and also links the tale with the possible intervention of supernatural evil, for the narrator reports that the lady was mortally wounded. However, since the regiment left immediately, he never did ascertain just how it all ended. Thus the mystery is heightened, and motivating circumstances are removed from the exposition of the anecdote itself. The narrator's final remark of assertion that all tales of ghosts are of this type underscores a rational basis for the supernatural.

This anecdote is now complicated by the emergence of a certain listener claiming to be a member of the very family in question, who states that the mother is still alive, and that it was not she who led the soldiers dressed as apparitions into the room, but an actual ghost which has from that time remained in the castle. The narrator's paled expression indicates that even though he claims nonbelief, he has now taken this twist of the story seriously.

The narrator is even more upset by the statement that all those who relate this story die within two weeks after the tale is told. Iriney Modestovich now outlines the unfortunate narrator's physical suffering as a result of the suggestion that he might die in two weeks. And so it allegedly happens, for Iriney Modestovich's final report is that in exactly two weeks there was one guest less at the home of Mar'ya Sergeevna. This statement, of course, is purposefully ambiguous and serves to strengthen the mysterious nature of events as well as to provide possible supernatural motivation for the ghostly visitation. For the moment the reader is left without an explanation for this extremely strange occurrence.

One of the travellers, a division chief, now relates an anecdote concerning a certain employee of his who went mad, hid in the division archives and declared that he was a "resolved case." This tragic-comic story serves to separate and extend the mysterious nature of the preceding events. Finally the frame narrator's question concerning whether the man had really died within two weeks is answered by Iriney Modestovich's glib reply:

69

I never said anything like that.[33]

Thus the previous suggestion of supernatural interference is negated, and the story comes to a close.

All of the anecdotes in this tale receive either definite or strongly clued rational motivation. Supernatural elements are constructed primarily as a joke upon or test of a character who challenges the otherworldly. Perception of ensuing supernatural encounters is always rendered from the point of view of the character who experiences the transnormal event, and narrators are typically estranged from those events which they describe. The absence of an eyewitness narrator serves neither to corroborate nor deny the true nature of events. The frame narrator, however, presents the author's point of view and asserts rational basis for the supernatural. Odoevskiy's story is a delightful parody on the many complicated yarns, effusive narrators, and intersecting narratives so common to this category of supernatural tale.

Like Odoevskiy, N.V. Gogol' contributed many tales of the otherworldly which fall into various categories. Typical of the supernatural anecdote is "The Fair at Sorochinsy,"[34] in which the alleged transnormal occurrences are rationalized as ruses perpetrated upon unwitting peasants. This tale revolves around the intrigues of a young peasant, Gritsko, who wishes to marry the fair Paraska in spite of the objections of her parents, Solopy and Khivra Cherevik.

The tale itself is structured so as to comprise thirteen chapter segments, each of which plays a role in the composition and rationalization of supernatural elements. The first chapter establishes the setting, a hot August day in the Ukraine, with peasants on their way to the Sorochinsy Fair. Chapter two completes this festive picture of the rather chaotic atmosphere at the fair and establishes the peasants' inclination toward belief in the supernatural through the delineation of an encounter between Paraska and her suitor whom she takes for the Evil One. There follows the tale of the district clerk who claims to have encountered the Devil in the form of a pig. This lends support to the rumors which soon circulate concerning the Devil who is allegedly present at the fair in search of his red shirt. Gritsko now proposes to Paraska, a suggestion which is summarily rejected by her father, and the scheming peasant connives with his gypsy friends to force Cherevik's consent to the match. Meanwhile, Paraska's mother is busy in an assignation with the priest's young son, Afanasiy Ivanovich. The appearance of Khivra's husband and his friends forces the startled Afanasiy into hiding. The peasants gathered in the cottage soon turn to talk of the supernatural, and the cossack Tsibulya relates the story of a devil who was kicked out of Hell. This yarn is interrupted by the appearance of a fenestral pig face and the hasty retreat of those present. Cherevik and his wife escape from the gathering in a panic. Chapters ten and eleven detail the supernatural joke played upon poor Cherevik and his friend Tsibulya by Gritsko and his gypsy friends. Chapter twelve completes the rational motivation for this encounter. Paraska and Gritsko are married, and the tale concludes with the entire company engaged in frenetic whirling and dancing.

The supernatural is initially introduced through inference and is linked with one of the first meetings between Paraska and her suitor whom she takes for the Devil:

> She thought that someone had given a
> tug at the embroidered sleeve of her
> blouse. She turned around and saw
> the bright-eyed young man in the white
> sweater standing before her. She
> trembled and her heart throbbed like
> never before at any joy or grief. It
> seemed to her that something both won-
> derful and strange was happening, and
> she herself wasn't able to figure out
> what was happening to her.[35]

Peasants discuss the decision of the location for the fair and conclude that it is to be held on an evil spot. The story of the district clerk's encounter with the pig's face gazing out of a barn window is related by another peasant in the form of hearsay. Thus the peasants reveal themselves to be superstitious believers in supernatural phenomena.

The initial supernatural event is introduced in the form of rumors that the Devil's red jacket had been seen among the wares at the fair. This is immediately followed by the old peasant woman's alleged encounter with the Devil in the shape of a pig bending over the wagons as though searching for something. The manifestation itself is constructed from the point of view of the old woman:

> An old bread-seller fancied that she saw the
> Devil in the form of a pig continually bending
> over the wagons as if searching for something.[36]

The narrator, however, adds that the old woman had been helping herself to the wares available at the neighboring drinking booth and could not walk a straight line. Even though exact

71

motivation for this occurrence is not provided, rumors, in combination with the inebriate state of the ignorant old peasant, provide strong rational motivation for this manifestation of the supernatural.

Tsibulya's anecdote is prefaced by the narrator's remark
that everyone would have thought it a sin to disbelieve the old
woman's story. The peasants, huddled together in the cottage,
are unaware that they have interrupted the amorous activities of
Khivra and her lover, who is now hiding precariously in the loft
above their heads. The narrator notes that night was falling.
Thus the characters' agitated emotional state and environmental
circumstances unite in support of the appearance of supernatural phenomena. Tsibulya's anecdote is in fact preceded by his
scoffing challenge to the Devil:

> Even if it were the Devil--who's the Devil?
> Spit on him! If he stood here before me
> this very minute, I'd rather make a long
> nose at him, damn me if I wouldn't.[37]

The scene is now set for a test of a nonbeliever, and Tsibulya's
claim is put to the trial by rejoinders from other members of the
assembled gathering. The visitors' spirits rise as the bottle is
passed around the table. The participants are now depicted in
an inebriate state and are conditioned for an encounter with the
netherworld.

Tsibulya's tale of the Devil going about the marketplace in
the shape of a pig collecting scraps of its jacket is interrupted
by a rattle at the window:

> The rest of the sentence froze on the speak-
> er's lips: there was a loud rattle at the
> window. The panes fell tinkling on the
> floor, and a pig's face, terrible to look
> upon, stared in at the window, rolling
> its eyes as though asking 'What are you
> doing here, good people?'[38]

The anecdote is constructed so as to interrupt and coincide with
the events in the main narrative. The mystery is therein
heightened, and the narrator's assertion of skepticism at the supernatural is put to the test. The peasants, already terrified by
the sudden appearance of a fenestral pig face, are sent into complete panic by the unfortunate Afanasiy Ivanovich whose tumble into the room is interpreted as an onslaught by the Devil himself.

Chaos is the result as Tsibulya and Cherevik are left unconscious on the road outside the cabin where the storytelling occurs. Finally, the confounded peasants' lapse into unconsciousness is linked with their alleged confrontation with the Devil in
the form of a pig.

The machinations of this devil-pig may be rationally explained since the tall gypsy present in the room is probably that
same tall, sunburned gypsy who had earlier concluded an agreement with Gritsko. Therefore the reader suspects that the appearance of the pig face may be part of an elaborate ploy ar-
ranged to frighten Cherevik into relinquishing his daughter in
marriage.

Cherevik now believes that the Devil is indeed present at
the fair collecting pieces of his red jacket. A scrap of red
cloth is found in his belongings and is given to Cherevik as a
towel by his wife. The moment of perception is depicted from
Cherevik's point of view with the exclamation:

> Oh horrors! A piece of the red sleeve of the
> sweater![39]

The Devil's red jacket is also linked with a third appearance of
the tall gypsy who questions Cherevik concerning his wares.
Cherevik now attempts to lead his mare forward and discovers
yet another piece of the red jacket tied to his severed bridle.
Perception of the ill-fated red sleeve is again rendered solely
from Cherevik's point of view:

> Here Cherevik would have pulled at the bridle
> to lead his mare forward and convict the shame-
> less slanderer of his lie; but his hand moved
> with extraordinary ease and struck his own
> chin. He looked--in it was a severed bridle,
> and tied to the bridle--oh horror! His hair
> stood on end--a piece of the red sleeve!
> Spitting, crossing himself and brandishing
> his arms, he ran away from the unexpected
> gift faster than a man half his age, and van-
> ished into the crowd.[40]

This scene is followed by Cherevik's capture and constraint for
the theft of his own mare. There follows the natural rationalization for the appearance of the red jacket as the tall gypsy
collects his reward from Gritsko. Thus the alleged appearance
of the Devil's wearing apparel may be attributed to the gypsy's
joke upon a befuddled and unsuspecting peasant.

It is not difficult to conclude that "The Fair at Sorochinsy" is similar to other tales of its type. This is true of the construction of transnormal episodes and also of the rationalization for the supernatural which seems to be uniform for this category. The supernatural is introduced in the form of rumors and hearsay. In this story, however, there is no direct contact with a supernatural being, and the supernatural is linked with the sudden appearance of pig faces and a bit of wearing apparel attributed to the Devil. All of the comic manipulations in this tale may easily be rationalized as part of a charade perpetrated upon the unsuspecting Cherevik. In addition, Tsibulya's anecdote is constructed as a typical test of an individual who scoffs at the possibility of the supernatural and who is subsequently rebuffed. Others who experience the otherworldly are depicted as inebriated or in an altered emotional state. All of those who encounter the supernatural seem prone to a lapse into unconsciousness. This presents the possibility that alleged supernatural occurrences are hallucinations, which serves to strengthen the mysterious aspect of events.

The construction of supernatural episodes serves neither to support nor deny the veracity of each encounter. The actual moment of initial encounter with the supernatural is depicted from a point of view internal to the character experiencing the transnormal event. At the moment of manifestation the consciousness of the narrator merges with that of the character experiencing the supernatural and expresses his point of view. The subsequent reactions of individuals who feel that they have indeed encountered the Devil are constructed usually from a point of view external to these characters themselves through a process of cataloguing their physical responses. The reader learns, for instance, that Tsibulya:

> sat petrified with his mouth open. His eyes were almost popping out of his head like bullets. His outspread fingers stayed motionless in the air.[41]

His friend Cherevik:

> clapped a pot on his head instead of a cap, dashed to the door like a scalded cat, and ran through the streets in a frenzy.[42]

The reader, witnessing the reactions of a character in the throes of an encounter with the otherworldly, nonetheless draws his own rational conclusions from clues carefully implanted within the narrative.

74

We have shown that this second type of supernatural tale is subject to definitive compositional laws. Supernatural anecdotes are treated both humorously and seriously but are always rationalized as jokes or cases of mistaken identity involving an ironic test of a character who claims that he does not believe in the supernatural. If outright motivation for the supernatural is not present within the narrative, there are within each anecdote clues and hints which strongly indicate rational bases for all allegedly transnormal occurrences. Narrators of these supernatural anecdotes always seem spatially or temporally estranged from the events which they describe and are not generally those who originally experienced the uncanny events in question. Those who tell of brushes with the otherworld are shown to be uneducated, unenlightened, superstitious folk or children who naively espouse belief in the supernatural.

Those who experience the terror of these ambiguous encounters are depicted as emotionally aroused, drunk, torn by passion, or grief-stricken. Within this story type the supernatural being is most commonly an animated corpse of a man or the ghost of a woman. In addition the range of supernatural powers is expanded to include monsters and animated inanimate objects. These otherworldly creatures are not only seen and heard by their victims but are touched and smelled as well. The supernatural power may in fact not appear at all but may exist only according to rumor. An encounter with the supernatural is constructed from the point of view of the victim who experiences this altered state, and such an event is followed by a lapse into unconsciousness or sleep. An omniscient eyewitness narrator is never present except to corroborate a rational explanation for events.

An atmosphere of mystery is developed through extensive environmental shading, and these anecdotes of the otherworldly are so constructed that rationalization for events is presented only in retrospect. Suspended or interrupted narratives serve also to intensify the mysterious nature of events and support the pervasive authorial contention of nonbelief in the supernatural. In fact, it may be said that within this story type supernatural encounters are always linked with the expression of a moral principle or spoof upon the unenlightened. Ever present within these tales is the basic premise that "supernatural" phenomena do not really exist, and that alleged occurrences of such phenomena are always rationally motivated. Expressed in digressions, asides, and in an ironic tone, the basic authorial contention is that reality itself always forms the basis for the supernatural.

Russian writers of supernatural tales were not to confine themselves to tales framed as dreams or anecdotes which present this rather restricted point of view. "The Fair at Sorochinsy" and to a certain degree "Alyonushka" serve as a transition to a third category of supernatural tale in which the supernatural acts occur directly within the narrative and are no longer framed as dreams or anecdotes, nor is their motivation firmly established. Gogol''s tale foreshadows an approach to the supernatural which was entirely new for Russian literature. The didactic function of supernatural elements now recedes somewhat and is replaced by a new philosophical perspective, an assertion that the supernatural may indeed exist. Yet it remains for each reader to decide this issue for himself.

Gogol''s young lovers whirl out of sight leaving behind an all-pervading empty and ambiguous silence which tempts one to pose Dostoevskiy's piercing questions, "Is anyone out there? Is there a living man in the field?" After all, even the pompous Tsibulya comments, "Even if it were the Devil. . ." It thus appears that in the deepest recesses of the old Cossack's uneasy heart there resides a touch of superstitious fear of some unrecognized and evil presence. So it probably is with us all.

FOOTNOTES

[1] "Kikimora" was first published in Northern Flowers for 1830. The text used for this study was Orest Somov: Selected Prose in Russian. Michigan Slavic Materials, No. 11 (Ann Arbor, 1974), 77-93.

[2] Ibid., p. 79.

[3] Ibid., p. 87-88.

[4] "The Cuirassier" was published in the journal Son of the Fatherland, Nos. 1-4 (1832). The text used for this study was A.A. Bestuzhev-Marlinskiy. Sochineniya v dvukh tomakh, I, 548-596.

[5] Ibid., p. 581.

[6] Ibid., p. 584.

[7] Ibid., p. 567-568.

[8] "An Evening at the Caucasian Waters in 1824" was first published in the journal Son of the Fatherland and Northern Archive, Nos. 37-41 (1830). The text used for this study was the above cited A.A. Bestuzhev-Marlinskiy. Sochineniya v dvukh tomakh, I, 234-290.

[9] Ibid., p. 246.

[10] Ibid., p. 247.

[11] Ibid., p. 254.

[12] Ibid., p. 256.

[13] Ibid., p. 253.

[14] Ibid., p. 258.

[15] Ibid., p. 277.

[16] Ibid., p. 285.

[17]V.A. Zhukovskiy (1783-1852) was a leading translator and poet of the early nineteenth century. It was in his translations of German and English poetry that a new literary current termed preromanticism was introduced into Russia. His two famous translations of Burger's "Lenore," entitled "Lyudmila" and "Svetlana," introduced the ballad of the supernatural into Russian literature.

[18]"Alyonushka" appeared in the 1837 edition of Vel'tman's tales, which was utilized for this study.

[19]Ibid., p. 10.

[20]Ibid., p. 37.

[21]Ibid., p. 66.

[22]Ibid., p. 62.

[23]Ibid., p. 66.

[24]Ibid., p. 70.

[25]Ibid., p. 71.

[26]Ibid., p. 76.

[27]Ibid.

[28]Ibid.

[29]"The Apparition" was written in 1834 and appears in V.F. Odoevskiy. Romanticheskie povesti (Leningrad, 1929), 202-214.

[30]Ibid., p. 203.

[31]Ibid., p. 206.

[32]Ibid., p. 212.

[33]Ibid., p. 214.

[34]"The Fair at Sorochinsy" forms the first tale of Part I of Evenings on a Farm Near Dikanka. The author worked on the tale during 1829-1830. Utilized for this study was the N.V. Gogol': Sobranie khudozhestvennykh proizvedeniy, I, 20-56.

[35]Ibid., p. 27.

[36]Ibid., p. 38.

[37]Ibid., p. 39.

[38]Ibid., p. 43.

[39]Ibid., p. 49.

[40]Ibid.

[41]Ibid., p. 44.

[42]Ibid.

CHAPTER FOUR

THE VEIL OF TERROR

Thus far we have examined tales which contain supernatural elements framed as dreams or anecdotes. Such stories not only receive rational motivation but seem intended to debunk belief in the existence of supernatural phenomena. A third category of supernatural tale presents transnormal events which are aimed both at rational and supernatural motivation. Within this particular story type supernatural elements are no longer framed as dreams or anecdotes but occur directly within the narrative. The reader is faced with ambiguous events which remain ultimately unexplained. Final resolution for these occurrences is "veiled," which means that supernatural motivation for events is now suggested but is concealed. There remains also the possibility that alleged encounters with the supernatural are merely hallucinations of individuals experiencing altered mind states. Short stories which demonstrate this particular construction of supernatural elements are Pogorel'skiy's "Poppy-Seed-Cake Seller of the Lafyortov District," Pushkin's "Solitary Cottage on Vasilevskiy Island," "The Queen of Spades," and Gogol''s "The Overcoat."

Illustrative of the technique of the veiled supernatural is Pogorel'skiy's "Poppy-Seed-Cake Seller of the Lafyortov District,"[1] the story of a certain Onufrich, a retired postman, his wife Ivanovna and their daughter Masha. Onufrich's eccentric aunt, an octogenarian who sells cakes for a living, supplements her income by telling fortunes and is therefore suspected of involvement with the Devil. Ivanovna conspires to appropriate the old woman's wealth by marrying off Masha to the mysterious and feline Murlykin, a rather stodgy old fellow and an alleged figure from the underworld. Supernatural occurrences include a cat in human form, an animated corpse, and several visits by the ghost of the old cake lady herself.

The introduction to this tale establishes the old cake seller's nephew and his family in a new home. The old lady has died, and Onufrich, her only heir, has inherited the old woman's property. The tale then reverts to the past as the frame narrator relates the story of how the Onufriches came to acquire their new residence. The narrator reports that the events which he recalls occurred fifteen years before the burning of Moscow. This is an indication that the storyteller himself did not witness these occurrences but is reporting what was told to him in the form of hearsay. According to this narrator, certain neighbors charged the old cake seller with witchcraft and sorcery. Another reported her to the police for engaging in unlawful card divinations and for associating with suspicious persons. The narrator himself neither supports nor denies the veracity of these claims which are reported solely from the point of view of bystanders.

A subsequent police search reveals nothing indicating that the old cake seller had been engaging in any wrongdoing. The narrator remarks casually that the methods used by this old woman to prove her innocence were unknown. As a result it would seem that supernatural means might indeed have been employed. Another sign of a possible link between the old crone and evil powers is the series of unfortunate events which befall her accuser and his family. It is reported that the unfortunate man's son fell and poked out his eye. His wife also tripped unexpectedly, breaking her leg, and their best cow suddenly collapsed and died. The narrator chooses to attribute these accidents to "fate," but the precise cause for events remains veiled and ambiguous.

Also relegated to the sphere of rumor are the assertions of still other neighbors who claim to have seen a large crow with fierce burning eyes light on the old woman's house. Others were certain that the old fortuneteller's black cat which accompanied her every evening was none other than the Devil himself. These accusations remain neither supported nor denied by the narrator. Onufrich, however, seems convinced that his aunt is in league with the Devil, for he attempts to dissuade her from such associations.

The description of the old woman also receives dualistic treatment. She is reported to possess qualities of kindness and good will. Soldiers on guard where the cake seller trades love her because of the free cakes which she bestows upon them at the close of each business day. As a fortuneteller the old crone prophesies only good fortune and, lulled by this good news, visitors generously reward her as a seeress. The old fortuneteller may be an evil figure engaged in purposive deceit for her own benefit or she may be truly interested in the welfare of her clients.

The initial supernatural event is the appearance of a huge cat which assumes human form. This occurs as the old cake seller attempts to divine a bridegroom for her beloved niece. The apparition remains visually manifest but does not speak to the frightened child. This scene is described totally from the point of view of young Masha:

> Casting an inadvertent glance at the black cat,
> she saw that it was dressed in a green frock
> coat; and in the place of its former round head
> there seemed to her a human face which, screw-
> ing up its eyes, was staring straight at her.[2]

Previous incidents are constructed in order to indicate possible psychological motivation for this manifestation. During the divination scene Masha is reminded of everything that she had heard about the old woman's strange behavior. The impressionable young girl is frightened by the nocturnal atmosphere, the chiming of the midnight bell, and the twelvefold meowing of the cat, all of which is immediately followed by the old woman's strange action and incomprehensible words. It seems to Masha that the old cake seller is performing some sort of ritual. The young girl falls unconscious during the divination and awakens to find the room in its original order. Thus the supernatural event is followed by the victim's lapse into unconsciousness and may be linked with hallucinating or dreaming. The narrator contributes no further evidence which would indicate that this occurrence is motivated either rationally or from the world beyond.

A successive encounter with the supernatural occurs during the scene following the announcement of the old woman's death:

> Ivanovna and her daughter crossed themselves
> and bowed to the ground. But on their minds
> was the treasure which was awaiting them.
> Suddenly they both trembled at the same time.
> It seemed to them that the deceased was look-
> ing at them from the street and bowing to
> them! Onufrich and the policeman, who were
> praying with great zeal, noticed nothing.[3]

Perception now stems from the viewpoints of two characters simultaneously. This plurality of viewpoint is highly significant and indicates increasing objectification of the supernatural phenomenon. Extenuating this dual perception, however, is the distance of the apparition from Masha and her mother which may serve to blur their vision. A mutual hallucination is also possible, for it is reported that Masha and her mother were thinking of the treasure to be inherited by Masha after her marriage to the bridegroom of the old woman's choosing. This occurrence may also be equated with the expression of a moral lesson, that evil is the result of greed. The narrator is not an eyewitness to this event but only reports that neither Onufrich nor his guest saw anything because they were praying so fervently.

Depiction of the circumstances surrounding the death of the old fortuneteller is cast in the form of rumors and is described by a friend of the retired postmaster. Certain neighbors asserted that a strong wind raged about the old woman's hut even though elsewhere the weather was quiet. Onufrich's friend, claiming that he had heard all of this from another, saw nothing because he had overslept on the morning of the old woman's death. Rumors soon arose that dogs had gathered before the old woman's window and had howled along with her cat which had meowed frightfully. The friend of the friend of Onufrich also had reported that lights in a long row stretched from the cemetery to the old woman's house. Depiction of unusual noise, whistling, laughter, and shouting heard in the old woman's house is framed with the statement:

> They say. . .[4]

Thus reports of the death of the poppy-seed-cake seller are shrouded in rumor and hearsay often twice removed from the character chosen to report the event.

At the funeral of the old woman Ivanovna is stunned by what appears to be the animation of the corpse:

> When Ivanovna was bidding Auntie farewell, she suddenly jumped back, paled and trembled noticeably. She assured everyone that she was unwell, but after it was all over Ivanovna quietly confessed to Masha that it had seemed to her as if the dead woman had opened her mouth and wanted to grab her by the nose.[5]

No one else in the room witnessed the corpse's sudden movement, and the scene is described only in retrospect by Ivanovna to her daughter. The occurrence is rendered totally through the external appearance and internal reaction of Ivanovna. At no time is the narrator himself an eyewitness to the alleged visitation from the otherworld.

The old woman's ghost subsequently appears on the evening of the Onufriches' arrival at their newly inherited home. The manifestation of this apparition is once more described from the point of view of Ivanovna. Neither Masha, her father, nor the narrator is witness to this event:

> Suddenly she heard a rustle beside her, and someone tapped her lightly on the shoulder. She glanced around. . .behind her stood the dead woman wearing the same dress in which she had been buried! Her face was angry. She raised an arm and threatened Ivanovna with a finger. In terrible fear Ivanovna shrieked loudly.[6]

The ghost is now both audibly and tangibly manifest. Onufrich, however, sees only that his wife is pale as linen and trembling

all over. Perception from the point of view of a single character is maintained on the phraseological level by the statement:

. . .but Auntie again appeared before her. . .[7]

Use of the word "Auntie" indicates the point of view of Ivanovna
and not of the narrator.

The angrily threatening shade serves to reintroduce the allegorical issue and provides psychological motivation for the phenomenon as the possible result of Ivanovna's feelings of guilt.
Onufrich's assertion that if his wife would pray her hallucination
would cease serves to introduce the theme of Christianity as a
palliative against evil supernatural forces. Ivanovna notes that
as she herself becomes involved in prayer the apparition fades,
finally disappearing altogether. The existence of positive Christian supernatural forces is here implied, but no such forces are
visibly manifest.

The apparition now appears to Masha and is described from
her point of view with the statements:

It seemed to her. . .she heard. . .Masha
saw. . .[8]

repeated seven times throughout the scene. This particular
shade, however, is first depicted devoid of the usual horrific
form but is smiling. The amiable ghost disappears as Masha
forms the sign of the Cross, an act which reinforces the triumph
of Christian supernatural forces over evil powers. Possible rational motivation for this occurrence is also suggested and is
provided by Masha herself who indicates that the whole episode
may be the result of nothing more than the play of her imagination. The narrator neither supports nor denies either of these
possible explanations.

Masha now feels something lightly caressing her face. She
also perceives a mysterious presence walking about the room
breathing heavily. The frightened young girl becomes convinced
that her grandmother is shuffling about the room quietly calling
her name and attempting to jerk away the blanket. The apparition once again assumes a friendly pose and lacks the horrific
visage perceived by characters in previous encounters. The
door is opened and something or someone descends the stairs.
Finally Masha clearly sees her grandmother beckoning and
standing by the well with her cat. During the entire scene the
narrative proceeds from the point of view of Masha alone, and an
eyewitness narrator is again conspicuously absent.

The final supernatural element in the tale is the emergence of Masha's suitor in the form of her grandmother's cat. The appearance of this anthropomorphized cat is linked with another aspect of the tale's moral element, the assertion that money cannot buy happiness. Masha notices a resemblance between the rather feline appearance of titular councilor Murlykin and her late grandmother's pet. The confused young girl now remembers the old woman's command that Masha must marry the suitor who would make his appearance soon after her grandmother's death and disclose the secret of the old woman's occult art. Perception of the titular councilor in the form of a cat emanates from the point of view of the young girl:

> Father! It's grandmother's black cat, answered Masha.[9]

The mysterious suitor's family name, "Murlykin" (from the Russian "Murlykat'," to purr), in combination with his bent-shouldered appearance and burring speech are indeed catlike and provide possible psychological suggestion for Masha's suspicions. The final portion of this scene, Murlykin's flight from the house with a neighboring dog in hot pursuit, is also constructed from Masha's point of view and provides further psychological motivation for her belief in the supernatural animal. Onufrich's statement:

> Oh what an ignorant country girl you are![10]

underscores this psychological motivation and emphasizes the young girl's naive inclination toward belief in the supernatural. In the final analysis the interdiction of the old woman is disobeyed, for Masha rejects the feline Murlykin and is rewarded with the appearance of her true love, Julian. The destruction of the Onufriches' new home at the very moment of the young lovers' wedding remains an enigma, and the tale concludes with a toast to the happy couple.

Pogorel'skiy's story is significant for it was to represent a new attitude and orientation toward the supernatural, an emphasis upon the ambiguity of events which remain unexplained and dually motivated. Psychological motivation for alleged supernatural occurrences is possible because the narrative focuses wholly upon the external and internal reactions and expresses the point of view of victims who may be experiencing hallucinations. The narrator does not function independently during manifestations of the otherworldly, and his consciousness is seemingly affixed to these persons.

This story is unusual since concurrent supernatural motivation for events is also suggested. Now for the first time more
than one individual experiences the supernatural at a given
moment. This plurality of perception indicates the creation of a
new narrative device leading toward eventual objectification of
supernatural phenomena. In this case, however, dual perception
is extenuated by the narrator's comment that both victims of the
supernatural were preoccupied with the same thoughts at the moment of manifestation. Thus a mutual hallucination must also be
considered as a possible cause for events.

Supernatural motivation is plausible since a number of mysterious events within the tale remain subject to the possible intervention of evil powers. Examples of such occurrences are the
misfortunes which befall the neighbor who denounces the old fortuneteller, the mysterious cat, the strange appearance and behavior of Murlykin even noted by Onufrich, and the destruction
of the old woman's house at the very minute of Masha's marriage.
Could fate or coincidence alone explain these events satisfacto-
rily?

Also noteworthy within this tale is the introduction of the
Christian element and the allegorical construction of supernatural
episodes. The possibility that positive Christian supernatural
forces are powerful enough to contradict evil is strongly suggested and supports the supernatural motivation theory. This
tendency to balance psychological with supernatural motivation
for events is to be further developed and refined in Pushkin's
"Solitary Cottage on Vasilevskiy Island" and "The Queen of
Spades."

"Solitary Cottage"[11] is a little-known story which has sel-
dom been subjected to critical scrutiny. The tale possesses a
realistic framework from the initial description of Vasilevskiy
Island and the everyday life there of an old woman and her
daughter Vera. Through a delineation of the elderly matron's
attempts to locate a suitable groom for her daughter and in the
depiction of the old crone's mortal illness, the author presents a
realistic portrait of both female psychology and the individual
wrestling with the ambiguity of impending death. The tale also
accurately pictures late eighteenth-century society and mores
through the scenes at the Countess I.'s St. Petersburg salon,
which is described in detail. Realistic also is the presentation
of encounters which explore the psychology of human beings
driven to a frenzy by fear or passion. Into this real world are
introduced purported encounters with supernatural phenomena
constructed so as to receive both rational and supernatural motivation.

Vera has a distant cousin, Paul, who visits his relatives on occasion. Young Paul is guided about the world of high society by his friend Bartholomew, an alleged servant of the Devil sent to accomplish the destruction of his unsuspecting friend. Paul is invited to a mysterious soiree at the home of the aforementioned Countess I., where he fails to notice that the guests may be disguised devils. When Paul and Bartholomew argue, a supernatural force renders the young victim unconscious. Having fallen in love with the countess, Paul establishes a rendezvous with her. This meeting is interrupted by a malevolent stranger, and the unsuspecting Paul is driven off by a devil-cabby who commands carriage number 666. Forming the sign of the Cross, Paul is able to accomplish the disappearance of the cab with its horrific driver. The terrified hero falls into delirium and awakens at home three days later. Meanwhile the old woman dies. Vera falls completely under the evil influence of Bartholomew, and the cottage on Vasilevskiy Island burns to the ground under suspicious circumstances. Vera, believing that she may be responsible for the damnation of her mother's soul, soon follows the old woman to the grave. Bartholomew mysteriously vanishes, and Paul returns to the country in dementia.

The initial supernatural encounter within the tale is the ballroom scene at the home of Countess I. There are two plausible explanations for the fact that the guests at this event are distinguished by their high wigs and wide trousers, and choose not to remove their gloves during the entire evening. Perhaps they are not people at all, but devils whose tall wigs cover horns, and whose wide trousers and gloves mask claws and hooves. The guest described as the victim of a certain:

bodily insufficiency[12]

may be a grotesque devil. At least one critic assails poor Paul for not perceiving that this is indeed the case.[13]

Realistic motivation for the scene is presented in the explanation that the Countess had not long before come from foreign places, and that her manner of life was characteristic of those regions. This unknown place might be the netherworld or simply a foreign country. The question of motivation is strengthened by the statement that these customs do not agree with the fashions of Petersburg society known to Paul at the time. It is possible that these modes of dress seem unusual to Vera's naive young friend who is inexperienced in the manners of high society. The situation purports two plausible motivations which, when combined, enhance the element of mystery.

A second possibly supernatural situation is the bout between Paul and his shadowy cohort, Bartholomew, whom Paul has come to suspect as the cause for his troubles with the countess. The statement concerning Vera:

May an angel love the Devil?[14]

indicates that Paul has begun to associate Bartholomew with infernal powers. Bartholomew's reply that nature has not adorned them equally is ambiguous. Does Bartholomew here imply that he is not human, or simply indicate that their intellectual endowments are at variance? This argument leaves Paul in a rage. Such a frenetic state of mind leading to unconsciousness is common throughout all supernatural tales which we have examined thus far.

One blow renders Paul breathless and unconscious. The implication here is that such a shock might have required superhuman strength, for Paul regains his senses at the opposite wall, seemingly having been hurled across the room. Bartholomew has managed to exit, close the door, and utter something during this fleeting instant, all of which would be difficult for a normal mortal. Bartholomew's warning:

Quiet down, young fellow. You haven't
tangled with your brother, you know.[15]

is ambiguous. It may indicate that Bartholomew is not human, or may warn Paul that the two have now become adversaries. The event is so structured that it is impossible to ascertain whether a supernatural act has in fact occurred.

Possible supernatural motivation may be attributed to the incident which occurs when Paul returns to the countess' home a second time to restore friendly relations with her. Having achieved his aim, Paul returns to the scene of general activity and overhears one of the gamblers complain that he had lost several hundred "souls." The countess' immediate reprimand and indication that he should have said "rubles" intensifies this misstatement and strengthens the mysterious nature of the situation. Paul shrugs off the remark, but the mystery remains subject to dual interpretation. The gamblers may be devils playing for human souls or landowners involved in some sort of game for serfs, also termed "souls." The scene acquires a further supernatural configuration with the narrator's comment that all commotion ceased suddenly as if removed by the sweep of a hand. Once more we find dual motivational devices.

A successive link in the chain of possible encounters with the supernatural is provided by Paul's dream, which is motivated by the youth's spiritual agitation and excitement because of a proposed nocturnal assignation with the countess. The dream sequence, however, is not subjected to dual motivation but serves structurally to illuminate the young hero's psychological state by revealing the febrile condition of his fantasy. In this way the dream also provides realistic motivation for the successive encounter with the supernatural cabdriver. Two of the three dream sequences involve a serpent and are linked with Bartholomew as Paul's agitated thoughts continually turn to his erstwhile friend. Thus the dream sequence manifests the hero's increasing suspicion that he may be dealing with the Devil.

Contrasting motivations are also evident in the ensuing episode of the mysterious visitor who interrupts Paul three times during his nocturnal tryst with the countess. Following the second interruption Paul's command:

Send the stranger to the Devil![16]

may be interpreted as a mere expletive of exasperation but is also a link with infernal powers. After the third interruption Paul vows to ascertain what kind of "apparition" has appeared, but this interjection is followed by the assertion that it must have been a joke, indicating that Paul himself believes a prankster may have perpetrated the interruptions. Here we see the union of contrasting motivations function even in the depiction of the thoughts of various characters.

The sight of the cloak, the closing door, and the sound of the gate attribute rational motivation to the appearance of the mysterious intruder. Paul catches sight of a tall man disappearing down a side street. This dexterous individual seems human but also possesses the ethereal ability to appear and disappear at will. Supernatural coloration is underscored by the trebled repetition of the statement that the mysterious figure disappears or vanishes:

without a trace[17]

when a normal mortal would leave footprints in the snow. Paul is described as wading in snow up to his knees. The mystery now deepens, and the encounter closes with the ambiguous statement that Paul has managed:

to come to his senses.[18]

The entire episode is blurred as the possible hallucination of an individual wandering deliriously in the snow.

The snow-chase episode leads directly to Paul's fantastic midnight encounter with the devil-cabby. A frenetic state of mind, the delirious pursuit of the elusive stranger-apparition, the midnight encounter with the devil-cabby, the nocturnal atmosphere reminiscent of the ballads of Zhukovskiy, and the thoughts of dead bodies or of cabbies who murder their fares, link possible rational motivations for an encounter with the supernatural. The catalyst for this reaction (Paul has already shown himself to be psychologically impressionable) is the cabby's tin badge imprinted with the apocalyptic number 666.

The scene of this encounter is constructed from Paul's point of view:

> In the light of the moon he wanted to get a
> good look at the cabby's tin badge and, to
> his amazement, he noticed that on this badge
> there was no indication of a unit or block;
> but in large figures of a strange form and
> cast there was written the apocalyptical num-
> ber 666, as he later recalled.[19]

The statement, "as he later recalled," indicates that the narrator is reporting retrospectively what he was told by Paul. This technique of separating the depiction from the occurrence allows for the blurring of time and indicates possible hallucination or fabrication on the part of the individual experiencing the phenomenon. Thus the role of the narrator as a possible eyewitness is precluded. The detailed account of Paul's spiritual agony and the doctor's diagnosis that the young man's illness is mental and not physical support a rational explanation for the episode.

Supernatural shading is provided, however, by the apocalyptic number, the sign of the Cross, the wild laughter and the whirlwind followed by the sudden reversal of the scene and disappearance of the fantastic coach with the words:

> Everything merged with the snow. . .[20]

The repetition of the explanation:

> Quiet down, young fellow; You haven't
> tangled with your brother, you know.[21]

links the episode with Bartholomew and strengthens the reader's impression that Paul has fallen into the hands of evil. The question of how Paul manages to make his way beyond the city gate, where he is found in a delirious state, remains unanswered. It is unlikely that he could wander so far in a raging blizzard, and the mystery deepens.

The animation of Vera's deceased mother forms the fifth supernatural encounter. This supernatural act is preceded by a
series of motivational elements subject to dual interpretation.
Supporting realistic motivation for the supernatural appearance
of the mother is the highly emotional state of the young woman.
Frightened by Bartholomew's demand for immediate allegiance to
him in deference to her own soul, Vera is intimidated by his assertion that no one can defend her from his power. Hypnotized
by Bartholomew's glance and the dim light of the room, the half-
crazed girl could imagine that she sees her mother raise an arm
and wave toward Bartholomew:

> . . .and Vera thought that she saw two rays
> of fire flow from his eyes, and it seemed that,
> in the flickering light of the candle which was
> going out, the dead woman raised her head
> with indescribable torment and with a withered
> hand waved her toward Bartholomew.[22]

Thus the internal perception of Vera is indicated and an eyewitness narrator able to substantiate the occurrence is not present.

Supporting possible supernatural motivation is Bartholomew's
demand that Vera swear allegiance to him, a request reminiscent
of selling one's soul to the Devil. Also mysterious are Bartholomew's promises of miracles in a faraway kingdom, his assertion
that no force can defend Vera from his power, and his penetrating stare which seems capable of animating the corpse.

Bartholomew's face expresses:

> powerless evil[23]

when Vera falls to her knees before the Cross. This may indicate the powerlessness of the Devil before God or may result
from the frustration of an insecure and passionate man attempting to win the object of his affection. The narrator's statement
that Vera now knows with whom she is dealing indicates that the
young girl is at last convinced of Bartholomew's infernal origin.
Perhaps Bartholomew himself believes that he possesses supernatural powers, for he is described as:

> frenzied.[24]

Vera's lapse into unconsciousness follows the pattern requisite
for those who purportedly experience supernatural phenomena.
The young victim's plunge into unconsciousness also links the
encounter with possible dreaming or hallucinating.

Although Vera remains convinced that Bartholomew is a visitor from Hell, the image of this frenzied man suffering from a headache, tormented by passion, and biting his lips in frustration seems equally mortal. Bartholomew may indeed be a visitor from the underworld, but he is also a deranged mortal with delusions of grandeur. The compositional principle of presentation of dual motivation for supernatural events is preserved.

The conflagration scene concludes the chain of possible supernatural occurrences. The narrator's hint that the flaming curtains were a gift to the old woman links the episode with Bartholomew and with the supernatural. Natural causes for the fire are also established since it is reported that a servant had placed a candle at the head of the deathbed. This candle is about to sputter out as Vera sees the vision of the animated corpse. With both Vera and the servant unconscious and Bartholomew absent, the curtains may have ignited from the candle.

Supernatural motivation is strengthened in the narrator's report that the fire boiled up with redoubled fury to singe the old servant woman's hair. This act is accompanied by her senseless flight into the other room. Such a state of mind is common to people who experience supernatural phenomena.

The description of the efforts to extinguish the fire is factual, evidencing a return to realistic narration. This verisimilitude is evidenced by the remark that firehouses were not in general use at that time. However, an immediate flight into the fantastic is apparent in the statement once more personifying the fire as having:

despised[25]

the efforts of the firemen. The appearance of a satanic visage follows one of the firemen's attempts to extract the body of the old woman from the flames:

> He told that he had just succeeded in making
> his way to the bedroom and was just about to
> approach the dead woman's bier when suddenly
> a satanic visage sprang up,. . .[26]

The alleged encounter is qualified by the statement:

He told. . .[27]

delineating the point of view of the fireman narrating a story in retrospect. The absence of an eyewitness narrator is again indicated. The supernatural nature of this event is mitigated also by witnesses who note that the would-be rescuer is a coward, and that a falling log seemed to him to be the Devil. Realistic motivation for the fireman's experience is further strengthened by the humorous description of his amplified stories of a devil with a tail, horns, and aquiline nose blowing up the flames like a blacksmith's bellows. Ironic references to the corporal as "eloquent," "a genius," and to his fellow drunks as "enlightened listeners" also support the entire occurrence as the result of a florid imagination. The glass of wine served to this corporal at the close of his performance is also established as a probable cause for his fantastic inventions. The theme of heavy imbibing is introduced here as a possible realistic explanation for supernatural events. Once more the structural principle of alternating modes of narration and motivation occurs with resulting dual interpretation and heightened mystery.

The structural principle of balance between supernatural and rational motivation continues throughout the denouement. No definite rational or supernatural motivation is provided for the events which have previously transpired. Bartholomew's disappearance acquires a possible supernatural hue, since he escapes during a time of year when navigation is impossible. Of course, the disappearance may also be rationally motivated since Bartholomew may easily have secluded himself.

The mysterious appearance of the tall blond man with green eyes is also linked with Bartholomew and possible supernatural intervention. The adjective "tall" had been attributed previously to the mysterious stranger who we assume is Bartholomew. The color of his hair and eyes has never been mentioned, but we assume that they are dark because of his imposing stance and penetrating glance. The mysterious visitor who alarms Paul may be Bartholomew, whom Paul in dementia mistakes for his erstwhile friend. The mystery and possibility for multiple interpretation remain.

The final elements of mystery also receive no resolution. The crazed behavior of Paul remains unexplained except for the narrator's reminder that Paul has a "flighty" nature. The secret of Vera's last year remains unresolved. A variety of terms implying mystery--"secret" ("taynyy"), "concealed" ("sokrovennyy"), and "mysterious" ("tainstvennyy") form a leitmotif underscoring this atmosphere.

The narrator presents a final demonstration of the balance between the real and the unreal, concluding with a rhetorical question concerning devils who interfere in human affairs. This indicates that the narrator himself believes in the supernatural motivation of events. His final explanation, however, ironically renders the tale more rationally motivated. The narrator reports that he has received the story orally through several members

96

of the Petersburg middle class. Thus the tale has been reduced to the interpretations of those who neither participated in nor witnessed the events described. The story is first presented as having taken place several decades previous to the time of the narration. This principle of removing the narration from the event described is illuminated above in the narrator's remark concerning Paul's encounter with the devil-cabby. Fantastic amplifications of events in retrospect are demonstrated by the corporal who purportedly relates his story until the end of his life with many fantastic additions.

The ironic final outcome of this story presents an interesting structural feature. This twist of fate is accomplished by Vera's refusal to marry Paul, her death, the ensuing retreat of Paul into the country, and his insanity followed by an untimely demise. Thus the possibly supernatural forces which are depicted as being powerless before acts of Christian ritual now triumphantly bring about the destruction of the hero, and the story ends tragically.

In addition to the principle of balanced motivation for supernatural events, a system of supernatural shading is infused into the real world of the narrative. This supernatural coloration applies both to the portrayal of characters and to the environment. The author employs attributive terminology which links certain individuals with positive or negative supernatural forces. These supernatural shadings are qualified by the presentation of realistic motivational features.

This principle of supernatural shading balanced by realistic designation is manifest in the characterization of Bartholomew. Supernatural coloration is evident in both his physical description and movement. Bartholomew extends Paul a "cold" hand of greeting. His countenance:

> did not reflect a soul like a mirror but like a
> mask concealed all its movement.[28]

He is branded "insidious," "sly," "evil," "a ferocious snake," and his laughter is "hellish." Further supernatural coloration is specified through the elaboration of exits and entrances. Bartholomew, described as "appearing from nowhere," vanishes three times when pursued by Paul during the chase scene, only to vanish altogether at the close of the story.

Bartholomew is depicted as being in possible possession of supernatural powers. He displays knowledge not normally accessible to humans. During the divination scene Bartholomew's knowledge of previous events so frightens the old woman that she purportedly forms the sign of the Cross. The scene is mitigated, however, by the narrator's observation that he is not certain about exactly what was said. The precise nature of Bartholomew's disclosures remains mysterious, providing the possibility for realistic motivation.

Throughout the narrative Bartholomew is linked with the Devil. Paul's remark that he will not go to Hell because of the means by which his friend garners money, is an early equation of Bartholomew with the underworld. This connection is supported by the statement that Bartholomew never attends the Orthodox Church. The immediate rejoinder that Paul is not often there either negates the extraordinary nature of the previous remark. The word "sacred" is linked negatively with Bartholomew by Paul's remark:

I know that for you nothing is sacred.[29]

Bartholomew is depicted as laying an evil snare for Vera through possibly supernatural means. This connection is established by placing him outside a church where he casts a watchful and suspicious eye upon her. This gaze disarms the girl and shatters her pious thoughts. Bartholomew claims ignorance of Vera's age because he did not "christen" her and has never christened anyone, but he is careful to assert exact knowledge of the ages of all with whom he is on familiar terms. This rejoinder is a possible indication of supernatural knowledge.

The interaction between Bartholomew and the old woman also underscores a link with the forces of evil. Bartholomew flares up in anger at the suggestion that a priest be called for the old woman. He becomes agitated when Vera cries out:

In heaven's name I implore you, do not leave Mother to die without confession.[30]

Bartholomew will not give his word of honor and trembles at the mention of the name of God. Indeed, he seems to be preventing the old woman from receiving the last rites of the Church. However, his answer that the dying woman might give up hope if a priest were summoned remains a valid excuse.

The narrative also receives supernatural shading through links between other characters and supernatural powers. The countess is termed "charming," "to the destruction of the descendants of Adam." The term "temptations" is also linked with the countess. Vera is "virginal," "innocent," and "angelic."

Paul is described as a sinner in the abyss of debauchery recal-
ling the path to salvation. Such references are subtle delinea-
tions of the biblical creation theme. The above designations are
veiled hints and receive no final resolution in fact. The characters believe that they are dealing with the Devil, but the paral-
leled presentation of mitigating factors extenuates this possibility
and maintains a harmonious balance between the real and the unreal.

References to supernatural themes or episodes from other
literary sources provide further supernatural shading. Bartholomew's entrance during his meeting with Paul is equated with the
marble quietude with which the statue of the commander arrives
at Don Juan's for supper. The scene is balanced with realistic
coloration through the statement that Bartholomew's countenance
soon acquired a more human expression. The ensuing concern
for his friend evidences a human and a sympathetic side to Bartholomew's nature and further qualifies the supernatural suggestion provided by the reference to Don Juan's unearthly guest.
Paul's midnight taxi ride is linked with the supernatural atmosphere of the ballads of Zhukovskiy, and Bartholomew's impas-
sioned request that Vera swear allegiance to him is reminiscent
of the Mephistophelian theme of ransoming oneself to the Devil.
However, the immediate reference to powerless evil depicts Bartholomew as a frustrated mortal and moderates the previous
supernatural suggestion.

Thus we may say that the principle of veiling the supernatural is maintained throughout this tale. Events occuring within
a real world have both supernatural and realistic motivation, with
all supernatural manifestations veiled and never resolved. Each
supernatural occurrence is reported by a single character in an
overwrought state of delirium, madness, drunkenness, or dreaming. No eyewitness narrator is present. Reports of supernatural events are separated from the time of the occurrence with the
result that the tale itself is finally placed within the sphere of
rumor and hearsay. The narrative is also constructed upon a
principle of qualified supernatural shading manifest through depiction of the physical attributes and actions of the characters,
the environment, and references to supernatural situations in
other literary works.

The technique of the veiled supernatural is applied also in
"The Queen of Spades,"[31] a tale of cabalism and madness, in
which the hero, Herman, is led to believe that an elderly countess is privy to the secret of a winning card combination. He
determines to extract this secret from her, but during their nocturnal confrontation the countess suddenly dies. At her funeral
a rather guilt laden and agitated hero fancies that the corpse

smirks at him from the coffin. Later the ghost of the old countess appears to Herman and divulges the long-sought secret.
Following the instructions of the ghost, Herman indeed accom-
plishes two miraculous wins with his first two cards. Playing
the third card, however, he loses, having turned up the queen
of spades instead of the intended ace. It seems to Herman that
the queen winks and smiles to him mockingly. Struck by the
resemblance between this queen and the old countess, the hero
goes insane and is committed to a mental institution.

The tale is constructed in such a way that both psychological and supernatural motivation for events are present within the
narrative. Supernatural suggestion is accomplished initially
through the anecdote narrated by Herman's friend Tomskiy who
tells of a miraculous win accomplished by his grandmother. Tomskiy, of course, was not a witness to this event which occurred
sixty years previous to the time of the narrative. This transfer
of the actual event into prehistory from the point of view of the
main narrative removes the supernatural event into the realm of
hearsay and rumor. It remains impossible to verify whether anything unusual really occurred. The tale of the miraculous win
is followed by unresolved debate on the possible existence of
supernatural phenomena. Rational motivations of luck and
marked cards are suggested but are denied by Tomskiy himself
who remarks:

I don't think so.[32]

Thus the mystery is intensified through this arcane hint which
may indicate the involvement of supernatural powers.

Escalating psychological motivation for Herman's alleged
transnormal experiences is present from the onset of the narrative, for the young man is depicted as the possessor of strong
passions and a fiery imagination. The story of the three magic
cards reportedly made such a strong impression on him that Herman could think of nothing else for a whole night. As he strolls
near the old countess' home, Herman's imagination is again fired
through contemplation of its mysterious owner and her ability to
divine winning cards. Upon returning home the nervous young
man is unable to sleep for some time. Playing cards, a green
table, heaps of banknotes, and piles of golden coins appear to
him in his dreams. Thus Herman's mounting obsession with the
fantastic card trick provides increasing psychological motivation
for his encounters with the otherworldly. The actual presence
of supernatural powers, however, is suggested in the narrator's
statement that some unknown force seemed to attract Herman to
the old house.

Environmental conditions maintain the hero in a heightened emotional state. Herman quivers like a tiger as he awaits the appointed assignation with the elderly countess. Howling wind, deserted streets, and large snowflakes underscore a surreal atmosphere and maintain the excited hero in an elevated mental state. The old countess' room with its accoutrements from the eighteenth century seems very strange to Herman. This mysterious atmosphere is underscored also by the narrator's reference to Montgolfier's balloon and Mesmer's magnetism.

Supernatural coloration is attributed to the scene through the description of the old woman who sits, all yellow, rocking as if under the action of some strange galvanism. Another link with the supernatural is Herman's assertion that the old countess' secret is connected with some terrible sin, with the loss of eternal bliss, or through some contractual arrangement with the Devil. Tomskiy's statement linking Herman with Mephistopheles is yet another indication of supernatural shading.

The initial encounter with the supernatural occurs at the funeral of the old countess during which the corpse glances up mockingly and winks at Herman. This encounter is foreshadowed by the narrator's statement that Herman could not silence the voice of his conscience which repeatedly labeled him as the murderer of the old woman. The narrator also reports that Herman was extremely superstitious and believed that the dead countess might be able to exercise harmful influence over him. Therefore, Herman's superstitious nature and guilt complex may well motivate the alleged encounter as the figment of an enflamed imagination.

These preparatory statements are linked with the narrator's description of Herman immediately prior to the appearance of the animated corpse. The young hero is in an extremely agitated state of mind and is described as:

Pale as the dead woman herself.[33]

The sudden animation of the corpse is constructed wholly from Herman's point of view with the statement:

It seemed to him. . .[34]

This particular manifestation is visual only, and the corpse is described as winking in a jocular fashion and glancing mockingly at the agitated young man. The church is filled with people, but Herman is the only individual of those assembled to experience this brush with the otherworld. The narrator is not an eyewitness to this ghostly animation but perceives events only through the consciousness of Herman who is probably experiencing a hallucination. However, the narrative provides no absolute motivation for this event.

There follows the visit of the old countess' ghost which appears to Herman on the night of the old woman's funeral. The animated corpse has already served as a source of emotional agitation for poor Herman whom the narrator describes as exceedingly troubled the whole day. Herman's alleged heavy drinking provides further psychological motivation for the ensuing visitation as a hallucination. The narrator also reports that the time of the manifestation was shortly after a quarter to three in the morning. Thus the moment of the supernatural encounter is linked psychologically for Herman with the exact time of the old woman's death which must have occurred at approximately the same hour.

The narrative proceeds with the indication that somebody in the street glanced in the window and darted away, but that Herman paid no attention to the incident. In reporting an event which Herman does not see, the narrator now emerges as an eyewitness who maintains his own independent point of view. Who is this "someone?" The narrator does not label the mysterious face in the window as the ghost. Perhaps the arcane visage is someone who accompanies the "ghost" on her nocturnal mission. Herman's officer friends may be playing a trick on him. Perhaps the story of the late countess' miraculous win is a fabrication intended to spoof the impressionable young man. The countess herself, immediately prior to her demise, when queried by Herman reports:

> It was a joke. I swear to you! It was a
> joke![35]

We have seen that the presentation of alleged supernatural events as a joke is common to the anecdotal type of construction discussed in "An Evening at the Caucasian Waters in 1824," "The Fair at Sorochinsy," "The Apparition," and "Alyonushka." The difference in this tale is that the usual clarification of motivation is not present, and the joke theory is but one of several plausible causes for events.

Herman initially is unsure of the identity of the apparition. Perhaps the ghost is the old countess' feeble housekeeper forced against her will to participate in a charade. She is the same age as the old countess and walks with great difficulty, which would necessitate accompaniment on the journey and would explain the characteristic shuffle of the shade.

102

Also significant is the fact that the ghost, unlike the countess in her meeting with Herman, addresses the young man in the
familiar form "ty":

> --I have come to you against my will, she said
> in a firm voice,--but I have been ordered to
> carry out your request.[36]

Thus the ghost may not be the countess at all. The old maid-
servant, however, might well use such a form in addressing
young Herman. Various explanations for the appearance of the
ghost may be submitted, but the compositional principle of veiled
motivation is preserved.

Psychological motivation for the phenomenon is supported by
the depiction of events primarily from the point of view of the
protagonist. The initial sound of the door opening, for instance,
is marked with the statement:

> He heard the door into the front room being
> opened.[37]

The appearance of a woman in white is marked also from Herman's point of view. The initial thought that this was his old
wet nurse is an indication of Herman's confused state of mind
and supports the theory that the vision may be the result of an
inflamed imagination.

The moment of perception that the old woman is indeed the
old countess' ghost is constructed also from Herman's point of
view and is marked with the statement:

> But the woman in white glided in and sudden-
> ly appeared before him,--and Herman recog-
> nized the countess![38]

The ghost is manifest audibly and visually but not tangibly. The
absence of tertiary sense perception underscores a slight estrangement between Herman and the ghost, maintaining the ambiguity and mysterious nature of this occurrence.

The disappearance of the apparition is depicted realistically as the ghost shuffles laboriously and is forced to utilize the
door for its exit. The fact that the orderly continues to lie
asleep on the floor indicates that Herman alone has experienced
the visitation. The mysterious nature of this phenomenon and
the possibility of supernatural motivation is supported by the
statement that the door into the hall remained locked. Subject

to a number of motivational interpretations, the event remains veiled and ambiguous.

The final fantastic animation of the queen of spades is perceived totally from Herman's point of view:

> At that moment it seemed to him that the queen of spades screwed up her eyes and sneered at him.[39]

The ensuing exclamation:

> The old woman![40]

emanates also from the perception of the hero. The episode is therefore subject to rational interpretation as a hallucination. There remains, however, the miraculous double win. In addition the gamblers' remark:

> A great punt![41]

is also ambiguous and may indicate the involvement of supernatural powers. Are these gamblers referring to the aplomb with which Herman dispatched his losing card, or do they acknowledge some sinister power present at the table which has tipped the cards against the hapless protagonist? The tale remains subject to interpretations which list both psychological and supernatural cause for Herman's various encounters with the otherworldly.

Critics have come forth to support one or another possible motivation for events. There is, for example, the proposition that all allegedly fantastic events are the result of drunken hallucinations.[42] This theory illustrates psychological motivation for the ghost's reported three-seven-ace series in Herman's contemplation of becoming the lover of the eighty-seven-year-old countess. The numbers three and seven are repeated throughout the depiction of Herman's ruminations. Other critics have attempted to discern psychological cause for the appearance of the ace which is not present within Herman's contemplations. The ace ("tuz"), for example, may be connected with Herman's subconscious desire to be a "big shot" (another meaning for "tuz").[43] It has been shown that a gambler beginning with a stake of one dollar makes successive wins of three dollars and seven dollars.[44] In addition, the numbers one, three, and seven, and verbs indicating trebling and increasing sevenfold were terms in common usage by card players at the time.[45] There is also the sugges-tion that the ace and the queen of spades become somehow stuck together, resulting in Herman's undoing.[46] All of these theories would support realistic motivation for all alleged supernatural encounters.

On the other hand, there is the theory of supernatural mo-tivation based upon the derivation of specific numbers associated with the cards themselves and with the sequence of play. It is suggested that the numbers one, three, and seven were believed to have magic powers. One is identified with God, "power, domi-nance, creativity, and independence." Three is associated with "creation, generation, perfection (the Trinity), and completion." Seven is the number most carefully associated with magic and is linked with the phases of the moon as well as with the rhythms of life.[47]

Within this theory one must pay attention to the order of play of the magic cards. A three plus seven equals ten, one, or unity, "a complete and perfect number." The sequence of play, first a three followed by the seven and ace includes numbers which possess increasing power of divination. The ghost seems to know that the ritual will be effective only if the cards are to be played on successive days. Thus one might conclude that the secret of winning cards must be of supernatural origin.[48]

Another critic emerges in support of the supernatural theory of motivation by examining the gambling, narrator, ghost, and Faust legend sign systems which are isolated from within the story. Objectification of the supernatural phenomena is attained through delineation of the ghost scene from two different view-points in combination with Herman's proven sobriety at the mo-ment of manifestation of the apparition. The psychological theory of motivation does not account for the determination of the third winning card, the ace. It is also difficult to explain psycholog-ically why Herman makes a mistake on the third night and con-fuses the ace with the queen, cards which possess radically dif-ferent designs.[49]

In addition one may isolate links between the Faust legend and Pushkin's creation in which Herman fulfills the triple roles of St. Germain (the midnight groom), the angel of death, and seeker of occult knowledge. In this scheme the old Countess also assumes the role of Mephistopheles through revelation of occult knowledge to Herman. Assuming also the role of the angel of death, she appears at the card table as the queen of spades.[50]

Within this perspective it is necessary to note the sinister tone of the final gambling scene culminating in Herman's tragic loss. The circle of gamblers may be controlled by St. Germain. The chief gambler, Chekalinskiy, seems to maintain a mysterious relationship to evil powers, and the other players seem also to possess certain arcane knowledge of events culminating in Herman's downfall. This is evidenced in their remark, "Great punt!" ("Slavno spontiroval") which may suggest the mystical presence of St. Germain himself who punts the last time and calls forth the old countess who mocks at Herman.[51] Thus the tale remains subject to interpretations and reinterpretations which include both psychological and supernatural motivation for poor Herman's alleged encounters with the otherworldly.

We may summarize then that "The Queen of Spades" provides one anecdotal supernatural encounter in combination with three examples of supernatural phenomena which occur directly within the narrative and are motivated possibly by the psychological state of the hero and possibly throgh the actual intervention of supernatural powers. Tomskiy's story of his grandmother is removed into prehistory, and definitive rationalization for the secret of the winning cards is intentionally left ambiguous by the author. Instead incidences of transnormal encounters possess possible psychological motivation as hallucinations stemming from Herman's frenetic mental state. Further psychological motivation for his encounter with the supernatural may be attributed to visions engendered by heavy imbibing.

On the other hand, the interference of otherworldly powers is suggested through supernatural shading of the environment, mysterious remarks, references to strange forces and galvanisms, implied links between certain characters and infernal powers, cabalistic enumeration, and Herman's surprising win against the odds. In addition, the emergence of an eyewitness narrator just previous to the moment of manifestation of the old countess' ghost lends further ambiguity to the situation. Herman is perhaps the victim of a hoax, or he may indeed be the recipient of a message from the Beyond. Numerous interpretations for events remain within the realm of possibility, and the reader is left to ponder all of this for himself.

Another tale which is constructed in the fashion of the veiled supernatural in comic dress is Gogol''s "The Overcoat."[52] This story concerns the mode of life and eventual death of a minor civil servant, Akakiy Akakievich, whose sole aim in life is the acquisition of a new overcoat. Unfortunately, on the first day that he is able to wear his new possession, the coat is stolen. Thoroughly demoralized, Akakiy catches cold and dies. Subsequently his ghost returns and attempts to steal a coat from the Very Important Person, a high official who had refused Akakiy's pleas that he help in locating the stolen garment.

The fantastic elements of this tale are separated stylistically from the remainder of the story and are presented initially in the form of rumors that the corpse of a clerk searching for his stolen overcoat had taken to appearing at night. The technique of blurring is utilized in the story of the departmental clerk who had allegedly seen the ghost shaking a finger threateningly at him. The frightened clerk thought he had recognized Akakiy Akakievich, but ran off so quickly that he was not able to get a good view of the apparition, only glimpsing the phenomenon from a distance. This episode is reported from the point of view of the clerk who may be the victim of mistaken identity. The clerk's aroused emotional state is, of course, linked also with this manifestation of the supernatural. Final motivation for the occurrence is not provided within the narrative.

The comic tone of these episodes is apparent in the police orders to catch the ghost at all costs:

> dead or alive, and to punish him in the most
> cruel fashion as an example to others.[53]

Further blurring is evident also in the story of the policemen about to snatch a corpse by the collar when the dead man sneezed and disappeared, leaving the captors wiping their eyes. As a result the representatives of the law were not certain just what they had captured. One suspects that this "corpse" is all too lively and that the gullible policemen have been duped by their own superstitious naivete. Exact rationalization for this event is not provided within the story.

The Very Important Person's encounter with a ghost is subject to prior psychological conditioning. The narrator reports that the Person was a rather kindly fellow who had been haunted by the image of the poor clerk whom he had scorned. This emotional agitation is further indicated in the statement that the official was so moved that he sent another clerk to ascertain just how Akakiy Akakievich was getting along. The response that Akakiy had died in fever and delirium made a great impression upon him. The Very Important Person's conscience reproached him, and he was depressed all day. Thus the appearance of a ghostly visitor receives possible motivation as a hallucination induced by guilt.

The description of the Very Important Person's activities on the day of the encounter place him into that frenetic mind state common to those who encounter supernatural phenomena. There follows an additional source of motivation in the statement that the rather agitated official drank a few glasses of champagne at dinner. The excitement of visiting his lady friend, Karolina Pavlovna, also intensifies this emotional agitation and further en-flames his imagination. In addition, description of environmental conditions contributes to the formation of an atmosphere condu-cive to the appearance of supernatural phenomena. For instance, the wind gusts with veritable supernatural force and lifts the Very Important Person's collar above his head.

Finally, during the actual ghostly encounter the following markers indicate the point of view of the Very Important Person and signify the absence of an eyewitness narrator:

> The Very Important Person felt. . .He
> noticed. . .He recognized. . .He saw[54]

The coachman, on the other hand, saw or heard nothing apart from the frightened commands of his client.

The ghost is manifest both visually and audibly:

> It was not without horror that he recognized
> Akakiy Akakievich. The Civil Servant's face
> was white as snow and looked like that of a
> dead person. But the horror of the Very
> Important Person increased considerably when
> he saw the mouth of the deceased twist up, and
> exhaling the dreadful breath of the grave,
> Akakiy's ghost uttered the following words
> 'Aha! So here you are! I've--ah--collared
> you at last!. . .'[55]

The Very Important Person is greatly influenced by this visage, and his conduct is changed as a result of the experience. The reader, however, wonders if this apparition who reeks of the "terrible breath of the grave," is not a mortal in disguise. Nevertheless, this occurrence of the supernatural is depicted as rendering a moral effect upon the greatly subdued official.

The final occurrence of the supernatural is also couched in the form of rumors that the ghost of the dead clerk continues to appear in remote parts of the town. The ghost's appearance to a Kolomna sentry is described by the narrator as hearsay. The description of this sentry who is knocked off his feet by a pig shows him to be a buffoon whose word may be doubted. In ad-dition, the description of a tall, moustached ghost displaying a fist reveals the apparition to be more mortal than ethereal.

In spite of the reader's suspicions concerning the true nature of all these allegedly ghostly visitations, there is no final rationalization for events which are introduced either in the form of rumors or which are described by a narrator who reveals only hearsay. All alleged transnormal phenomena are delineated from the point of view of the character experiencing events which are often blurred. However, possible psychological motivation is provided in the frenetic emotional state of a character such as the Very Important Person who is aroused by guilt, heavy imbibing, and emotional agitation. The apparition conveys a didactic message, a reminder of retribution for evil and responsibility for one's actions.

We conclude then that an examination of supernatural elements within this story type yields a number of similar constructional principles. Of primary importance is the problem of motivation for alleged supernatural events. Psychological rationalization for encounters is strongly indicated, but there remains the possibility of concurrent supernatural intervention. This supernatural motivation is veiled or concealed, and encounters with transnormal phenomena receive no definite resolution within the narratives themselves. The problem of mystery is thus handled through presentation of narrative events which remain unsolved.

Realistic elements predominate in the actual depiction of encounters with the supernatural. The sequence of visual followed by audible and tangible perception of supernatural beings becomes less rigidly applied. Within this category audible perception may precede visual awareness of a supernatural figure, and there is a tendency toward the absence altogether of tangible contact between the mortal and his otherworldly visitor. This blurs and lends greater subjectivity to the phenomenon. In addition, the moral element is present but is placed into perspective and does not emerge as the dominant authorial consideration.

Encounters with the supernatural are preceded by careful delineation of the psychological condition of the character who is to experience the transnormal phenomenon. The resulting indication is that the individual is perhaps experiencing a hallucination engendered by an agitated emotional state, drunkenness, or madness. The narrative focuses upon the external and internal reactions of those characters experiencing the supranormal state. There are no witnesses among other members of the cast even though such individuals may be present at the time of the manifestation. Anomalous in this respect is the appearance of a ghost to two characters simultaneously ("The Poppy-Seed-Cake Seller"). Here the two individuals are depicted as possessing similar thoughts and a commonly agitated emotional state. Also irregular is the eyewitness narrator who sees the face in Herman's window ("The Queen of Spades"). It must be noted, however, that depiction of the ghost itself is maintained solely from Herman's point of view.

A broadening in perception and the occasional emergence of an eyewitness narrator support the possibility of supernatural motivation for events, a tendency which is to culminate in a new story type. The veiled supernatural, however, is mitigated by tragic and comic irony and by concurrent psychological portrayal of characters as human beings subject to the ambiguity of human experience. The result is a principle of syncrisis, wherein the supernatural coexists with the rational, and the stories themselves are subject to unresolved dual interpretation.

FOOTNOTES

[1] "The Poppy-Seed-Cake Seller of the Lafyortov District" was first published in 1825 in the periodical News of Literature. Utilized for this study was the text which appeared in Russkie povesti XIX veka 20-kh godov, II, 61-80.

[2] Ibid., p. 68.

[3] Ibid., p. 70.

[4] Ibid.

[5] Ibid.

[6] Ibid., p. 75.

[7] Ibid.

[8] Ibid., pp. 75-76.

[9] Ibid., p. 77.

[10] Ibid.

[11] When "The Solitary Cottage" first appeared in print, Pushkin's name was not mentioned. The tale was credited to a certain Titov who wrote under the pseudonym of Tit Kosmokratov. Titov later acknowledged that he had merely served as the amanuensis for the tale which actually belonged to Pushkin himself. The question of dual authorship of the tale is examined in detail by Kodjak who reconstructs and analyzes the intonations and sound gestures from Titov's record. Kodjak's findings indicate that the tale belongs more within the oeuvre of Pushkin than of Titov. Kodjak's article may be found in American Contributions to the Seventh International Congress of Slavists, II (Brown University Press, 1973), 321-337. The Russian text used for this study is found in Biblioteka velikikh pisateley: Pushkin, VI (Petrograd, 1915), 181-192.

[12] Ibid., p. 184.

[13] C.E. Passage, The Russian Hoffmannists (The Hague, 1963), 119.

[14] Pushkin, op. cit., p. 185.

[15] Ibid., p. 186.

[16] Ibid., p. 187.

[17] Ibid., p. 188.

[18] Ibid.

[19] Ibid.

[20] Ibid.

[21] Ibid.

[22] Ibid., p. 191.

[23] Ibid., p. 190.

[24] Ibid.

[25] Ibid., p. 191.

[26] Ibid.

[27] Ibid.

[28] Ibid., p. 191.

[29] Ibid.

[30] Ibid., p. 189.

[31] "The Queen of Spades" was first published in The Library for Reading, II, bk. 3 (1834). The text used for this study is found in A.S. Pushkin - Sochineniya, III (Moscow: 1954), 385-410.

[32] Ibid., p. 388.

[33] Ibid., p. 405.

[34] Ibid.

[35] Ibid., p. 399.

[36] Ibid., p. 406.

[37] Ibid.

[38] Ibid.

[39] Ibid.

[40] Ibid.

[41] Ibid., p. 410.

[42] This theory is suggested by Slonimskiy in "O kompozitsii 'Pikovoy damy'," Pushkinist: pushkinskiy sbornik pamyati S.A. Vengerova Ed. by S.V. Yakovleva, IV (1922), 171-180. A similar proposition is set forth by V.V. Vinogradov in Stil' Pushkina (Moscow, 1941), 558.

[43] J.T. Shaw, "The 'Conclusion' of Pushkin's 'Queen of Spades'," Studies in Russian and Polish Literature, ed. Zbigniew Folejewski et al. (The Hague, 1962), 119.

[44] Nabokov, ed., and tr., Eugene Onegin (New York, 1964), II, 261.

[45] Letter to Andre Meynieux, in Pouchkine, Oeuvres Completes, ed. Andre Meynieux (Paris, 1953-58), III, 500, fn. 5.

[46] L.V. Chkhaidze, "O real'nom znachenii motiva tryokh kart v 'Pikovoy dame'," Pushkin: Issledovaniya i materialy, III (Moscow-Leningrad, 1960), 455-460.

[47] See the article by N. Rosen, "The Magic Cards in 'The Queen of Spades'," Slavic and East European Journal, 19 (4, 1975), 268.

[48] Ibid.

[49]See another article by A. Kodjak, "'The Queen of Spades' in the Context of the Faust Legend," Alexander Pushkin: A Symposium on the 175th Anniversary of his Birth (New York, 1976), 109.

[50]Ibid., p. 89.

[51]Ibid., p. 110-111.

[52]"The Overcoat" was first published in the 1842 edition of Gogol''s complete works. The text used for this study is found in N.V. Gogol' - Povesti, III (Moscow, 1960), 174-218.

[53]Ibid., p. 213.

[54]Ibid., p. 216.

[55]Ibid.

CHAPTER FIVE

THE DEVIL AND HIS DISCIPLES

In our previous study we have examined Russian supernatural tales which are rationalized as dreams, jokes, hallucinations, or which remain unexplained and are subject to dual motivation. A fourth story category includes the nonframed direct narrative intrusion of supernatural powers. Transnormal phenomena now become wholly objectified since otherworldly beings are described by an omniscient eyewitness narrator who possesses conscious and independent perception of events. Numerous supernatural beings populate these stories, and the narratives may be constructed so as to express their own independent point of view. It was N.V. Gogol' alone who, contrary to the position established by his contemporaries, took this plunge into fantasy and expressed an open belief in the supernatural. Tales which best exemplify this story type are Gogol''s "A Terrible Revenge," "The Night Before Christmas," and "Viy."

"A Terrible Revenge,"[1] a grisly tale of murder, incest, and infanticide, best illustrates the transition to this story type. Previously established methods of constructing transnormal episodes are not abrogated entirely, but rational cause for the supernatural becomes less plausible, and supernatural motivation is in fact established through the presence of an independent eyewitness narrator.

The initial setting of the tale is a certain area of Kiev where the Cossack Captain Gorobets is celebrating the wedding of his son. As the captain raises the icons in order to deliver a prayer, all of the guests are horrified when an unknown Cossack in their midst is suddenly transformed into an evil wizard. After the celebration the captain's adopted brother Danilo, his wife Katerina, and young son sail homeward along the Dniepr River. On their journey the unsuspecting family suddenly encounters a bevy of animated corpses which rises from a cemetery located on the shore. The next morning Katerina's father comes calling and, criticizing the young couple's late return, deliberately initiates a fight with Danilo, wounding the young Cossack in the arm. Danilo later eavesdrops on his father-in-law whom he interrupts in the process of an incantation intended to evoke the soul of his daughter Katerina and force her to become his bride. Danilo now realizes that the old man is that same wizard who had appeared during the wedding ceremony.

Intent upon the destruction of the Russian Church, the evil old Cossack is subsequently imprisoned for plotting against the Russian Orthodox people but is freed by his naive daughter. Meanwhile, the Poles take action against the Russians, and Danilo is eventually murdered by his father-in-law who supports the Polish cause. There follows Danilo's funeral feast and the return

117

of the wizard whose ensuing incantation is interrupted by the ominous appearance of a lofty vision in a cloud which fills his cave. Undaunted by this forewarning of vengeance, the wizard allegedly murders Katerina's child and drives the frenzied young woman to madness. A miraculous knight now appears, quickly dispatches the wizard, and the tale ends with an old bandura player's song reinforcing the theme of retribution for evil.

The narrator's initial descriptive statement:

> There was a hustle and bustle in a certain
> part of Kiev. . .[2]

establishes the characters who populate this story in frenetic activity conducive to the appearance of supernatural powers. However, the notation:

> In the old days[3]

is an indication that the original tale occurred many years previous to the present narration and allows for the possible blurring of time, establishing a possible hearsay basis for the narrative.

The narrator's additional assertion:

> . . .they loved good fare but they liked drink-
> ing still more. . .[4]

links imbibing with the subsequent occurrence of the supernatural, although such a descriptive statement serves probably to provide couleur locale and may not explain the appearance of the wizard since not everyone who witnesses the alleged supernatural event has been drinking. In addition, the scene in which the newlyweds are blessed before the icons and the narrator's statement that no evil power dares approach the man in whose house they stand establishes the possible presence of positive as well as negative supernatural forces.

The moment of metamorphosis of the Cossack into a wizard is described from the point of view of the narrator:

> When the captain lifted up the icons, the Cos-
> sack's face suddenly changed completely. His
> nose welled up and twisted to one side. His
> eyes changed from brown to green. His lips
> turned blue, and his chin trembled and grew
> pointed like a spear. From his mouth there

appeared a tusk, and a hump jutted from behind his head, and the Cossack turned into an
old man. 'It's him! It's him!' the crowd shouted and pressed close together. 'The wizard's
shown up again!' mothers shouted and grabbed
their children by the hand.[5]

Such plurality of perception is not to be found within any other
type of supernatural tale which we have thus far investigated.
The narrator's description of the event lacks qualifying modals
and verbs of perception ("they saw," "they felt," "it seemed to
them," etc.) common to depictions of supernatural encounters in
other story types. Faced with the icons the wizard vanishes,
and the possible presence of mitigating positive supernatural
forces is reinforced. Such beneficial powers are rarely apparent
in other Russian tales of the supernatural.

The true nature of the uncanny appearance of the Cossack-
wizard remains subject also to various rational motivations. Description of the strange metamorphosis is followed by the narrator's assertion:

Almost everyone told about it differently, and
no one could tell for sure about him.[6]

As a result the event becomes more nebulous, and the reader
suspects that the occurrence may have been magnified through
rumor and hearsay. The ensuing statements that a barrel of
mead was rolled out along with many gallons of Greek wine, and
that the Cossacks dropped into a slumber everywhere around
provide further evidence for interpreting the alleged "supernatural" encounter as the result of inebriate misinterpretation on
the part of foolish and superstitious peasant folk.

The second supernatural encounter in this tale is the appearance of a series of animated corpses as the Cossack family floats
homeward down the Dniepr. In conformance with the usual pattern of describing a supernatural encounter, the author presents
environmental circumstances which condition the occurrence.
Katerina's expression of fear at the strange tales of the wizard
and Danilo's assertion:

'It's the wizard who wants to frighten folks so
that no one will dare to break into his foul
nest.'[7]

serve to form psychological prefiguration for the subsequent encounter and link this occurrence with the previous appearance of
the wizard at the wedding celebration.

The delineation of this second encounter with the otherworld also emanates not from the perception of a single individual but includes the reaction of many who witness the eerie phenomenon, including the narrator himself. The child's and Katerina's screams, the oarsmen who drop their caps in terror, and Danilo's shudder testify to this common perception of events. The narrator too perceives the grotesque apparitions, for he presents a horrific description of the three corpses with claws and twisted distorted faces. In addition, the storyteller's remark concerning a certain withered corpse:

> One could see that it was suffering terrible torments.[8]

reinforces the perception of an independent narrator who experiences events along with, yet separate from, the frightened Cossack and his family. The typical animated corpse motif is present here but lacks many of the usual rational resolutions common to other depictions of supernatural encounters to which we have become accustomed.

There follows the eavesdropping scene in which Danilo glimpses his father-in-law in the act of conjuring up Katerina's soul. The supernatural phenomenon is once more conditioned by environmental factors as the room is illuminated by transparent blue and gold waves of light. The initial transformation of the father-in-law into a wizard follows the more traditional pattern and is constructed from Danilo's point of view:

> Danilo began to look more closely. . .He looked into his face--and it began to change. . .and he saw before him that same wizard who had appeared at the captain's wedding feast.[9]

This description of the second appearance of the Cossack-wizard is accompanied by further environmental descriptions which include additions to the color spectrum (fading blue lights and a growing rosy light within the room combined with indications of the presence of moonlight, phenomena often linked with transnormal occurrences), and various audial data (ringing sounds, the murmur of wind). Finally, tangible environmental shading is added as Danilo perceives the chill of the night.

The vision of his wife's spirit is also transmitted solely from Danilo's point of view with the notations:

> And it seemed to Danilo that the cloud wasn't a cloud but that a woman was standing there[10]. . .Oh, it was Katerina![11]

As Danilo suddenly visualizes his own home, it seems to him that terrible faces peer out from the walls where the icons should have been. This would indicate the presence of evil powers which could not have been manifest in the sacred presence of icons. Finally the slumbering Cossacks whom Danilo passes on the way home indirectly link the encounter with dreaming. But Danilo has not been asleep, for he has been pulling at his moustache in order to assure himself that he is fully alert and awake. Even though this encounter is described from Danilo's point of view and is therefore unverifiable, dreaming must be eliminated as a cause, and supernatural motivation remains plausible.

The wizard too experiences a supernatural event as he mixes a strange brew deep in his cave. The scene of this vision, apparent within a white cloud which hovers in the cave, is described from the wizard's point of view:

> In the cloud before him there gleamed some
> sort of a miraculous face. . .Never before
> in his whole life had he seen anything like
> it. . .but then an overwhelming horror
> came over him. The strange marvelous
> face still glanced motionlessly at him
> through the cloud.[12]

Since description of this phenomenon is constructed solely from the point of view of the wizard, we must assume that the appearance of this strange apparition may be the result of a hallucination. Mysterious, supernatural configuration, however, is attributed by the final statement:

> Everything disappeared.[13]

The exact nature of this phenomenon remains unmotivated and ambiguous.

The scene of the death of Katerina's child also presents the possibility of supernatural intervention. Her father-in-law's statement that he would consult a wise woman against whom no evil spirit could stand links the scene with the possible interference of evil powers. A second link is formed by Katerina's prophetic dream in which the child's life is threatened by its grandfather.

Katerina now goes insane and is visited by a witch in the form of her nursemaid. The appearance of this supernatural figure is, of course, motivated psychologically, for Katerina is seen dancing and rolling her wild eyes. Perception of the nurse as a witch is rendered solely from Katerina's point of view through a series of interjections:

> You are terrible looking. There are iron
> pincers coming out of your eyes. Oh, how
> long they are! And they're burning like
> fire! You've got to be a witch![14]

The implied psychological motivation for this occurrence is mitigated by supernatural environmental coloration and also by the
narrator's suggestion that Katerina has refused to say her prayers, thus providing cause for possible evil supernatural intervention. Further supernatural coloration is attributed by the
narrator who notes that on such nights the souls of unbaptized
infants also clamber up tree branches. Constructed in the manner of the veiled supernatural, the event remains slightly vague
and is subject to dual interpretation.

Katerina is murdered the next morning. The timing of this
event violates the general formula for constructing supernatural
phenomena, which requires that transnormal occurrences take
place at night. Early in the morning a handsome visitor, clad in
a red coat, arrives at Katerina's house and inquires for Danilo.
This visitor expresses his sorrow when he learns of Danilo's
death, and at first Katerina is soothed by his manner. However, the crazed woman soon identifies him as her father, the
wizard, in disguise. Knife in hand, the frenzied girl hurls herself at the stranger and is killed in the ensuing struggle. The
narrator's hint that the visitor is wearing a red coat serves as a
prefigurative link with Katerina's father who has often been seen
wearing this same color. It remains unclear whether a supernatural event has occurred, however, because the alleged metamorphosis of the visitor into the wizard has been perceived by Katerina alone. The narrator seems to agree with this assumption
for he declares that the father has killed his mad daughter.

The following chapter details the appearance of a miraculous
horseman-apparition seen distinctly, even though at a great distance, by many people, including nobles and Cossack hetmans
who have assembled for the express purpose of witnessing the
marvel. The narrator too witnesses this miraculous phenomenon,
for he reports:

> The clouds vanished from the highest peak
> and on the top of it there appeared a horse-
> man, in full knightly regalia, with his eyes
> closed, and he was distinctly seen as though
> he had been standing nearby.[15]

The wizard not only catches sight of the apparition but is surprised to view the same face which had appeared earlier in his
cave. This moment of recognition is rendered strictly from the
wizard's point of view:

> Having glanced in terror at the marvelous
> knight, he recognized that same face which
> had appeared to him, though uncalled for,
> when he was working his spells.[16]

Subsequent events are related also from the point of view of the wizard but without the use of qualifying verbs of perception:

> He was about to leap with his horse over a
> narrow stream which lay across his path when
> his horse suddenly stopped at a full gallop,
> turned his nose back at him and, marvelous
> to say, laughed out loud.[17]

Although this passage is narrated exclusively from the point of view of the wizard, the words, "marvelous to say," indicate the presence of an omniscient narrator attributing his own exclamation of surprise at the phenomenon which he is witnessing. Succeeding perception of the trees nodding their heads and stretching out their limbs to strangle him is depicted again from the point of view of the wizard. Therefore, we find within this scene an initial supernatural phenomenon witnessed simultaneously by many different characters. Subsequent occurrences are constructed from a point of view which sometimes unites perception of a single character with that of the independent narrator. This extensive plurality of perception would indicate that something supernatural in nature may indeed have occurred.

In an attempt to seek prayers of forgiveness for his foul deeds, the errant wizard now flees to the holy places in Kiev and consults a holy hermit who perceives the letters in the scriptural passages dripping with blood. Because of this forewarning, the holy old man asserts that the wizard is beyond help. Enraged by this pronouncement, the evil figure attacks and kills the holy man. The wizard rides off in confusion and after several days once more encounters the miraculous horseman who, in one of the most horrific passages in all of Russian literature, takes final revenge upon him for his sinful acts.

The scene of the bloody scriptures is transmitted from the hermit's point of view through his statement:

> 'Look--the letters in the holy book are
> dripping with blood!'[18]

The narrator chooses neither to verify nor deny the validity of this occurrence. The subsequent appearance of the horseman-apparition, however, is depicted both from the point of view of the wizard and of the supernatural horseman himself. Initial perception of this phenomenon stems from the wizard and is expressed in these words:

> The clouds suddenly lifted, and before him
>
> there appeared a horseman in terrible
>
> majesty.[19]

At this point a shift in narrative focus occurs, and the evil wizard's final encounter with the supernatural horseman is depicted also from the point of view of the horseman-apparition through the following description:

> The motionless horseman opened his eyes
> and saw the wizard flying towards him and
> laughed.[20]

The supernatural horseman now emerges as an actively perceiving member of the cast, and the complete objectivity of this supernatural being is fully established.   The narrator also emerges to detail the agonizing death of the wizard, the resurrection of bodies from the grave, and grotesque corpses which leap to gnaw the flesh of the departed evil one.   Finally the story concludes with the old bandura player's tale which underscores the theme of retribution for evil.

Gogol''s tale includes elements of the veiled supernatural but also exhibits characteristics which place it within a new story type.   There is a marked increase in the number of otherworldly powers and perceptual viewpoints in the delineation of supernatural encounters.   The number of characters who experience supernatural phenomena now increases sharply.   Perception of these supernatural beings is often limited to the cognizance of a single individual, but the tendency is for broadening to occur, which results in the inclusion of many characters who witness supernatural phenomena simultaneously.   Most striking is the objectivity of supernatural phenomena achieved by narration from the point of view of the supernatural being itself, which is in turn perceived by many characters.

The gallery of supernatural beings is greatly expanded and, in addition to the animated corpses so typical to other story types, is broadened to include wizards, witches, souls, and apparitions of animals as well as of people.   Perception of these powers is apparent in the visual, audial, and tangible sensory areas.   Initial perception of the supernatural being may be either visual or audial, with tangible cognizance either subsequent or absent altogether.   The male gender predominates in the grotesque delineation of corpses, wizards, and apparitions, whereas the delineation of female supernatural powers is confined to depiction of the souls of women and children.

The problem of motivating supernatural phenomena is now resolved in a somewhat different fashion. There remains the tendency to depict transnormal occurrences as subject to psychological motivation such as the hallucinations common to insanity. Nevertheless, in several instances supernatural phenomena become totally objectified because otherworldly beings enter directly into the narrative, which may be constructed from their point of view, and are acknowledged to be of supernatural origin by the eyewitness narrator. As is demonstrated in many other Russian stories of the supernatural, thematic unity within this tale also exists in a pervasive authorial didacticism, the theme of eventual retribution for evil.

Also representative of the fourth story type, the direct narrative intrusion of supernatural powers, this time in comic dress, is Gogol''s "The Night Before Christmas,"[21] a delightful tale of devilry and love come true. The Devil himself and the witch Solokha are among the active members of the cast of this story which concerns the comic pursuits of the Evil One and others who attempt to win the objects of their affection. The Devil, caught in the act of wooing the desirable Solokha, is forced to hide in a sack in an attempt to avoid exposure. The blacksmith artist Vakula unknowingly carries off this very sack, and having consulted the portly oracle, Patsyuk, succeeds in forcing the Impure One to transport him to St. Petersburg where Vakula attends the court of Catherine the Great and manages to receive a gift of the Tsarina's slippers. Having returned home, the victorious blacksmith uses these slippers in an attempt to win consent of his request to marry the Cossack beauty Oksana. The tale ends with the report of their marriage and happy family life.

As is the case with "A Terrible Revenge," "The Night Before Christmas" includes supernatural beings which participate directly in the narrative and are described by a narrator who accepts their presence as natural and normal. Indicative of this orientation is the narrator's initial report that a witch astride a broomstick rode through the air gathering a sleeveful of stars. In addition, the narrator relates that the Devil succeeds in seizing and placing the moon in his pocket as if nothing had happened. The Evil One is rewarded for this attempt with a scorched hand, a reminder that even he is subject to retribution for such mischief. The narrator seems to be the only witness to this unusual atmospheric phenomenon, for he reports that hardly anyone in Dikanka noticed that the moon had been stolen. On the contrary, the district clerk perceived the moon dancing as he emerged from the local tavern:

on all fours. . .[22]

The absence of the moon is subsequently noted by the Cossack Chub and his friend Panas. The obvious tendency of these characters toward heavy drinking, however, is underscored by Chub's remark in reference to the village Sacristan's new cottage:

'There'll be some good drinking there now!'[23]

As a result, the reader may laugh off the episode as the hallucination of overimbibers. Yet the narrator is not intoxicated, and his eyewitness report lends a certain mysterious credence to this humorous event.

Completing the initial segment of this tale is the description of the Devil swearing revenge upon the blacksmith Vakula who has painted a mural in the church depicting St. Peter on the Day of Judgment. This is a further link with the expression of a moral concerning retribution for evil.

The narrator continues his objective report on the activities of the witch, Solokha, with the Devil in amorous pursuit. Solokha's witchhood has, in fact, been established only according to rumors spread by old women who drink too much. Such accusations are also supported by the cowherd, Timish Korostyavyy, who allegedly had seen Solokha with her hair down in the form of a witch milking cows. Timish had reportedly lain down to sleep immediately prior to this occurrence, was "spellbound" and unable to move. These facts, of course, imply psychological motivation for the cowherd's vision as a dream. In spite of all this, the narrator perceives the Devil and the witch as actual supernatural beings who participate directly in events, and he expresses no doubts concerning their validity.

Meanwhile, the Cossack beauty Oksana offers to marry Vakula if he is able to produce the very slippers which the Tsarina herself wears. In turn Vakula decides to consult the Zaporozhian, "Paunchy" Patsyuk who is known for his kinship with all sorts of devils. As the corpulent Cossack proffers advice, animated turnovers fly as if by magic into his mouth. This miraculous event is outlined both from the point of view of the narrator and of Vakula, as is the scene of the Devil hopping out of Vakula's sack and straddling the Cossack's neck. The Devil's thoughts and speeches are also reported by the omniscient narrator, and the hellish visitor's meekness forced by the sign of the Cross is an indication of the power of positive supernatural

forces which are allegedly present. Such powers are not manifest directly within this story either, but are felt primarily
through their effect upon the Devil, who is afflicted with fits of
sneezing and coughing at the appearance of the Cross which Vakula wears. These positive supernatural forces accompany the
blacksmith on his fantastic ride and seem to exert control over
the alleged forces of evil.

Vakula's miraculous ride to Petersburg on the Devil's back
is depicted from his own point of view. This fantastic adventure
is initially delineated as perceived by the blacksmith with the
words:

> At first it seemed frightening to Vakula when
> he rose up from the earth to such a height
> that he could see nothing below. . .[24]

The blacksmith's arrival in Petersburg is also depicted from Vakula's point of view through the statement:

> The blacksmith saw himself mounted on a
> fiery steed in the middle of the street.[25]

Narration from the point of view of the subject experiencing the
supernatural event combined with the rather peculiar descriptive
phrase:

> Vakula saw himself. . .

lead the reader to believe that Vakula may be experiencing a
dream or hallucination. However, the authenticity of this occurrence is soon verified by the eyewitness narrator who marvels
at the hustle and bustle of the big city:

> My goodness! The rattle, the uproar, the
> brilliant light; the walls rose up, four stories
> on each side; the clatter of horses' hoofs and
> the rumble of wheels echoed and resounded
> from every quarter.[26]

There follows an immediate return to the point of view of
the hero, and this scene is rendered by modals and appropriate
verbs of perception:

> It seemed to him as though all the houses had
> fixed their fiery eyes upon him, watching. He
> saw so many gentlemen in cloth overcoats that
> he did not know whom to take off his cap to.[27]

127

Vakula's subsequent encounter with some Zaporozhian Cossacks
on their way to visit the Tsarina is rendered also from his
point of view:

> Before Vakula had time to look around he
> found himself in front of a big house, went
> up a staircase, hardly knowing what he was
> doing, opened a door and drew back a little
> from the brilliant light on seeing the smartly
> furnished room.[28]

The ensuing delineation of the confrontation between the assembled Cossaks and the Tsarina is rendered realistically by an
omniscient narrator who presents successively shifting points of
view which include the Tsarina, Potyomkin, the Zaporozhians,
and Vakula himself. This scene of Vakula's audience with the
Tsarina is presented by a narrator who has eschewed his former
jocular tone of narration. This alternation in mode and shifting
focus of narration serve to objectify and verify the nature of
Vakula's fantastic adventure.

Finally, the dissolution of the scene is rendered again from
the viewpoint of the triumphant blacksmith:

> Vakula suddenly found himself outside the
> city gates.[29]

His return to the village occurs in the morning and is linked
with the crowing of the cock:

> And in an instant Vakula found himself near
> his hut.[30]

This return to everyday reality is linked also with Vakula's slumber in the hay until dinner. As a result, the description of the
blacksmith's supernatural journey follows the pattern typical for
the construction of supernatural episodes in which an otherworldly encounter is followed by the victim's lapse into the sleep
state. This would seem to indicate the possibility that Vakula's
fantastic encounter with the Devil and his journey to the court
of the Tsarina were the result of a dream. However, the blacksmith is in possession of the slippers and clothes which he had
obtained from the Tsarina and from the Zaporozhians on the previous evening. In addition, the narrative contains no indications
that Vakula is the object of a joke or a ruse. All of this serves
to negate realistic motivation for the occurrence, and the reader
is left only to conclude that a supernatural event indeed occurred. The tale now comes to a close with the happy marriage

128

of Vakula and Oksana, and the Devil instead of tricking others is spoofed himself.

What are we to make of all this good fun? Gogol''s tale contains otherworldly guests who appear to mortals visually, audibly, and tangibly. This pattern of manifestation conforms to other supernatural tales which we have examined. What is unusual here is that these allegedly supernatural beings appear to several characters at once. They participate actively in and manipulate a narrative which may be constructed also from their point of view. Not only are these beings now fully objectified, but they also seem capable of disturbing even the normal pattern of causal and spatial relationships. The Devil, for instance, is able to place the moon in his pocket and also may freely diminish his own size in order to fit into the witch Solokha's sack. Such events are perceived and transmitted by the narrator as normal. On the other hand, the presence of positive supernatural forces is not visually apparent, but their influence is indicated by the conduct of the Devil who cowers at the performance of various religious rituals. The tale, basically a humorous reminder of the eventual triumph of good over evil through retribution, supports the basic philosophical assumption that the supernatural indeed exists.

Among the most fascinating of Gogol''s works in the fantastic vein is "Viy,"[31] a horrific story of devastating supernatural intervention, which has been subjected to much critical speculation. Most scholarly investigations have centered upon the riddle of the tale's folklore sources indicated by the author himself in a footnote.[32] Typical in this respect is the work of Abaev,[33] who attempts to link the linguistic origin of the name "Viy" with the Indo-Iranian mythological demon-god "Vayu." Assuming another direction, Gramzina[34] assesses the tale according to social and historical bases. An interesting treatment of the supernatural in this tale is presented by Mann,[35] who presents an analysis of the fantastic within the framework of the somewhat broader context of the evolution of fantasy within the creativity of Gogol'. Mann concludes that the fantastic here is treated seriously but that such elements relate only to the past. Another critic, Driessen,[36] presents a definitive analysis of the role of the fantastic in the tale, but he pays little attention to the role of the narrator or to the function of point of view. A thoroughly incisive analysis of the purely supernatural elements in this tale is not to be found within the body of critical literature devoted to this work.

The tale itself consists of several episodic segments. The first of these includes the initial setting which places three Kievan schoolboys on their way home to spend the Easter holidays. Having lost their way, the boys find shelter with an old woman who purports to house them in various places. The second segment includes the somewhat uncanny encounter of Khoma, one of these boys, who is confronted by the old woman in the form of a witch riding on his back as if he were a broom. The subsequent segment includes Khoma's experience of reading prayers for the dead over the body of the daughter of a Cossack chief who, at the point of death, had mentioned the young student's name. Three nights in succession Khoma is forced to carry out this ritual. During the third reading a huge monster, Viy, appears. This shaggy creature, in the company of evil spirits, attacks the boy, and the youth dies. These spirits fail to flee from the church by dawn, and at the second crowing of the cock the evil spirits are caught hanging from the windows of the church. The story concludes with a statement detailing the activity of the unfortunate Khoma's friends and their discussion of the reasons for his untimely demise.

The initial supernatural element in this tale is Khoma Brut's encounter with the old woman turned witch, who has granted him and his friends lodging for the night. The delineation of this scene is preceded by two statements which hint at the students' penchant for heavy imbibing. The boys first approach the house with the hope:

> to get a little drink of something for the
> night.[37]

In addition, the old woman labels the students "drunkards" when they request food and lodging from her. As a result the boys' tendency towards excessive drinking is established in advance as a possible cause of an alleged encounter with the supernatural. However, there is no indication within the narrative that any such imbibing actually occurred immediately prior to Khoma's fantastic encounter, and this possible motivation remains without direct connection to the supernatural event.

Immediately prior to the appearance of the witch the narrator reports that young Khoma turned over on his side:

> . . .intending to fall into the sleep of the
> dead.[38]

Without indication that the protagonist has passed into the sleep state, the narrative now continues with the statement that the old woman entered the pen. It is significant that this moment of manifestation is rendered not from Khoma's point of view but from the point of view of the narrator who remarks:

> Suddenly the narrow door opened, and the old woman, bending over, entered the pen."[39]

This lends greater objectivity to the unexpected appearance of the witch.

The description of this scene with the young "philosopher's" unsuccessful attempts to push the old woman away, unable to lift his arms and legs, and not even in control of his voice indicates that Khoma is probably experiencing a nightmare. Dream motivation is also suggested in the statement that the old woman utters no sound. Yet if the hero is in fact dreaming, the moment of his passage into the dream state has been thoroughly masked and is not to be revealed retrospectively. This section is rendered from Khoma's perception with indications such as:

> The philosopher wanted. . .he noticed. . .he saw. . .he heard. . ."[40]

The ensuing depiction of the old woman leaping onto Khoma's back is also constructed from his point of view with the statement:

> He saw the old woman approach him, fold his arms, bend his head down, and with the swiftness of a cat leap onto his back. . .[41]

Repetition of the statement that the philosopher's legs now move independently lends further support to possible dream motivation for this occurrence. The moment of recognition that the old woman has been transformed into a witch is also rendered from Khoma's point of view and is marked by the exclamation:

> 'Hey, it's a witch!'[42]

The subsequent scene of the young philosopher galloping along with the witch on his back is rendered, surprisingly enough, from the point of the view of the eyewitness narrator who comments:

> Such was the night when the philosopher, Khoma Brut, galloped along with the mysterious horseman on his back.[43]

131

An immediate alternation to Khoma's point of view, however, ensues, and the depiction of a nymph swimming below is rendered through Khoma's eyes:

> He saw a water nymph swim out from behind
> some grass. . .She turned her face toward
> him, and her eyes were bright, flashing, and
> sharp. . .[44]

Khoma himself now questions whether he is dreaming. As a result the mystery of this episode is intensified, and the possible motivation for the fantastic ride becomes more blurred.

Khoma immediately gains control of the situation as the witch releases her grasp at the sound of the frightened boy's various prayers and exorcisms. The presence of unseen positive forces which have come to Khoma's aid is now indicated, and the boy springs up to leap upon the old woman's back. This twist of events is described from the point of view of the narrator:

> The old woman ran so fast that the horseman
> could hardly get his breath.[45]

Further description of this fantastic ride is accomplished from the spatial reference point of Khoma:

> The earth flew by beneath him. Everything
> was clearly outlined in the moonlight, although
> it was not a full moon.[46]

Finally, metamorphosis of the witch into a young girl is accomplished also from the reference point of Khoma:

> He stood up and looked into her eyes. Be-
> fore him lay a young beauty.[47]

Is Khoma's fantastic adventure simply the result of a drunken nightmare? At first glance the reader might assume this to be the case. However, the absence of evidence which indicates that Khoma has actually fallen asleep, the presence of a supernatural being subject to the control of Christian ritual, and the reports of an eyewitness narrator who emerges at significant points to corroborate events provide possible supernatural motivation for this episode which lacks final resolution.

There follows the account of the three nights of prayers for the dead Cossack girl. When Khoma is ordered to carry out this task, a strange foreboding envelops him. This event serves to prefigure the boy's ensuing encounter with evil powers. Khoma is also described participating in the Cossack merrymaking as the group approaches the estate where the boy is to take part in the funeral activities. The narrator notes that Khoma's legs felt like wood, and that he was unable to escape from the captivity of his Cossack hosts because the young inebriate saw so many doors that it was impossible for him to discover the right one. By the time of his arrival at the manor house Khoma could make out nothing distinctly and fancied that he saw a bear instead of the house. In this fashion the young hero is linked with heavy imbibing immediately prior to his initial encounter with the corpse in the church.

In addition, before being taken to the place of worship, Khoma is primed further with stories of the witchly activities of the deceased. The narrator reports that these stories of strange occurrences helped to work upon the young man's imagination. The narrator also indicates that Khoma fortified himself with one last glassful of vodka. Finally, when introduced into the church, Khoma at first yawns, an indication that he may be about to fall asleep. As a result the scene of the boy's initial encounter with the animated corpse is framed by subtle suggestion of possible psychological motivation for the supernatural visitation as the product of the heated imagination of a drunk.

Careful delineation of environmental circumstances also precedes the manifestation of the corpse. The black coffin, poorly illuminated by faintly glimmering candles, provides an environment which serves also to further pyramid the horrific atmosphere and act upon the imagination of the young hero. Khoma is subject to such suggestion, for his statement that the dead cannot trouble him because of his prayers, indicates that he indeed believes in the supernatural. The initial appearance of the animated corpse of the Cossack girl is preceded by interjections which provide the hero with further psychological suggestion:

> She's about to get up! She's going to rise! There! She's going to peer out from the coffin![48]

The deadly silence in the room, penetrated only by the sound of dripping wax, provides a final aura of mystery and horror.

The animated corpse is first presented visually with the statement:

> She raised her head. . .[49]

The pronoun "she," utilized ten times throughout the depiction of this scene, indicates the point of view of Khoma, whereas the use of the word "corpse" or "the young girl" would transmit the viewpoint of the narrator. Thus the initial appearance of the corpse remains uncorroborated by the narrator, and we may suspect that poor Khoma is experiencing another nightmare. In addition, the livid corpse threatening a terrified hero with the wag of a finger now introduces the tale's didactic element.

The narrative focus is soon to take a new twist, however. Description of the horrific bluish corpse gnashing its teeth and unable to cross the line marked off by Khoma is interrupted by the statement:

> Khoma didn't have the strength to look at her,[50]

and the narrator emerges as an eyewitness detailing a scene not fully perceived by the protagonist. The scene of the coffin suddenly breaking loose and beginning to fly whistling about the church is described from the point of view of the narrator. The final writhing and disappearance of the corpse is also detailed from the narrator's point of view:

> The corpse again raised up. . .The corpse lowered itself into the coffin and slammed shut the lid.[51]

Khoma is now in a state of frenetic excitement and fear, as is evident from the narrator's description of the frightened youth covered with sweat and with heart pounding. The hero now drifts into an unconscious state, and the horrific occurrence is framed with Khoma's long sleep. When the boy awakens, it seems to him that the events of the previous evening occurred in a dream. While dreaming or hallucination might seem plausible motivations for the encounter, there is no definite indication that Khoma was asleep during the episode, and the presence of an eyewitness narrator lends objectivity to the supernatural visitation.

The second night of reading over the corpse is initiated in much the same manner as the first. The narrator reports that Khoma was given a pint of vodka at dinner and in this fashion links also the second evening's activities with the hero's tendency toward drunkenness. The scene is once more delineated primarily from Khoma's point of view:

> He again saw the dark icons, the flashing
> frames and the familiar black coffin which
> was standing motionless in the middle of
> the church in threatening silence.[52]

Initial manifestation of the corpse is again visual, but this time
the scene is delineated from a point of view which unites the perception of Khoma with that of the narrator:

> The corpse was already standing before him
> on the very line and was peering at him with
> its dead green eyes.[53]

The words "corpse" and "already" indicate the perception of an
objective narrator who offers a commentary on the situation,
whereas "before him" indicates the spatial position and perception
of the protagonist.

Audial perception of this phenomenon is now added from the
point of view of the hero with the statement that Khoma:

> . . .heard the corpse again gnashing its
> teeth and waving its arms, desiring to
> grab him.[54]

The picture of the corpse standing and unable to see Khoma is
delineated from a viewpoint which combines the perceptions of
Khoma and the narrator:

> But, raising one eye slightly, he saw that
> the corpse was not attempting to catch him
> where he was standing and, obviously, it
> couldn't see him.[55]

The remark "obviously" ("kak bylo vidno") indicates the point of
view of the narrator who is offering his personal commentary
about this scene. The delineation of ensuing action now returns
to the point of view of the hero with the notation that "she" (indicating the corpse) began muttering hollowly through dead
lips.[56] Perception of the corpse's incantations, depiction of the
noise of many wings, and the beating of wings on the panes of
the church windows are constructed from Khoma's point of view.

> The philosopher in fear understood that she
> was making incantations. . .He heard wings
> beating against the glass of the church
> windows.[57]

135

The young student's pounding heart and greying hair at this point indicate his extreme emotional agitation, a mental condition possibly conducive to the appearance of hallucinatory phenomena. In addition, the boy's drinking habits are once more emphasized by his request for another pint of vodka. Khoma seems to believe in the verity of his supernatural encounters, for he tells the old Cossack that his daughter was in league with Satan. Once again the occurrence of the supernatural is prefigured by elements which would motivate the occurrence as the victim's hallucination or dream. However, the narrator's perceptions and comments lend credence to possible supernatural motivation for events.

The final scene in the church is also prefaced by careful prefiguration which provides possible psychological motivation for Khoma's encounters with the netherworld. The narrator, for instance, reports that on the morning of the third day Khoma and his friend consume no less than half a pailful of raw brandy. After some merry frolicking Khoma lies down and falls asleep on the spot, and the narrator reports that it required a whole pail of cold water to rouse the drowsy Cossack for supper. Further preparation for the appearance of a supernatural figure is provided by the narrator who reports on atmospheric conditions:

> It was a hellish night. Whole packs of wolves howled in the distance. Even the barking of the dogs was somehow horrifying.[58]

Description of this third reading proceeds along the same structural pattern as the preceding encounters. Khoma begins the reading, but this time the exorcisms, protective circle which he has drawn, and repeated formation of the sign of the Cross are to no avail. Simultaneous visual and audible manifestations of the corpse exacerbates the horrific impact of this scene. The sudden appearance of the corpse with its teeth knocking and lips twitching convulsively is reported from the point of view of the narrator:

> Suddenly in the silence the iron lid of the coffin burst open, and the corpse rose up. It was even more terrible than the first time. It's teeth knocked horribly against one another. It's lips twitched in convulsions and, screeching wildly, it poured out incantations.[59]

Verbs of perception are absent in this description as is phraseology indicative of Khoma's point of view or his position of reference within the room.

Description of the whirlwind which now envelops the church, the falling icons, doors breaking loose, and the multitude of monsters filling the room is also undertaken from the point of view of the narrator:

> A whirlwind swept through the church, and
> the icons fell to the ground. Broken pieces
> of glass came flying down from the windows.
> The doors broke loose from their hinges, and
> an innumerable multitude of monsters flew into
> the church of God. The entire sanctuary
> was filled with the dreadful noise of wings
> and the scratching of claws. They were all
> flying around and looking for the philosopher.[60]

The word "philosopher" here reinforces the objective narrator's point of view, and the statement that the last traces of intoxication had disappeared from Khoma's head negates the possibility that this occurrence is a hallucinatory fancy.

Statements providing the basic descriptive elements of this scene are rendered from Khoma's point of view:

> . . .he heard the evil spirits rushing around
> him. . . .He didn't have the strength to make
> them out. He saw only that there was some
> sort of enormous monster filling the entire wall.
> . . .They were all gazing at him, searching and
> were unable to catch sight of him. . . .
>   He saw that they were bringing in a huge,
> squat bandy-legged creature. Khoma noticed
> with horror that he had an iron face.[61]

The narrator does not corroborate what Khoma sees by emerging as an eyewitness during these portions of the scene. However, he does hear the command of the corpse:

> 'Bring Viy! Go and get Viy!'[62]

which is reported in direct discourse and is not linked with Khoma's perceptions. The subsequent command of the monster,

> 'Raise my eyelids. I can't see!'[63]

is reported also by the narrator in direct discourse. As a result, the storyteller seems to be indicating that there is more to this scene than the hallucinatory ravings of a terrified youth.

The climactic moment of confrontation betweey Viy and Khoma is rendered from a point of view which unites the perceptions of Khoma with those of the narrator:

'There he is!' cried Viy and pointed an iron finger at him. And all of them rushed upon the philosopher. Breathless he fell to the ground and right then and there his soul flew out of his body in terror.[64]

The portions of this narrative constructed in direct discourse represent the point of view of the narrator as does the choice of the word "philosopher." Use of "he" and "him" represent the point of view of the victim. Thus the moment of catastrophe is shared by the narrator and the unfortunate young man. This broadened narrative focus serves to objectify the supernatural event.

Khoma now dies of fright, and the scene comes to a close with the narrator's description of the church with monsters stuck fast in the doors and windows. This scene is certainly one of the most horrific in all of Russian literature, essentially because of the implication that evil supernatural forces not only exist but may indeed triumph. No longer is the supernatural event constructed totally from the point of view of the victim who may be accused of dreaming or hallucinating. Even after the hero's death the narrator continues to report on the activities of the evil powers in the church.

The tale now concludes with a description of the subsequent activities of Khoma's school friends who, upon hearing of their comrade's demise, make for a tavern to drink to his memory. Consequently, the Cossacks' penchant for strong drink receives one final reinforcement, and the story closes with bacchanalian conversation concerning witches.

It is not difficult to see that Viy represents the most pure example of its story type. We have now come full circle from the dream tales and anecdotes which present such definite proof that the supernatural does not exist. The animated corpse and monsters which appear in this story are manifest to the protagonist visually, audibly, and tangibly. Perception of these supernatural beings may reside in more than one area simultaneously (as is the case of the corpse which rises up hissing at the same time). This increases the horrific effect of the otherworldly visitation. The presence of positive supernatural forces is at first implied by the hero's performance of religious ritual which for a time maintains his safety against evil. However, in the final analysis even these forces fail, and the poor philosopher falls victim to the very forces which he has taunted.

138

The actual appearance of supernatural beings is prefigured by factors which would purportedly motivate the occurrence psychologically as the result of the victim's heavy imbibing, heightened imagination, or fearful belief in the supernatural. Occurrences of the supernatural are framed also by the victim's frenetic activity and are preceded by indications that he may be sleeping. However, there is no clear proof that the victim is dreaming at any time during these encounters. In fact, the supernatural visitations are described both from the viewpoint of the victim and also from the perceptions of an eyewitness narrator who emerges at climactic points in the narrative to clarify what the hero may not perceive clearly due to his agitated frame of mind. It is this broadening in the narrative focus which provides final objectification of supernatural phenomena.

We may summarize then that Gogol''s stories of this type may be both comic and serious in nature and tend to employ an increasing gallery of supernatural powers, expansion in the number of characters who experience supernatural phenomena at one moment, a broadened narrative focus, and basic authorial position of support for belief in the supernatural. It is interesting that positive supernatural forces are not visually apparent, but their influence is felt in the actions of evil powers who sometimes submit to acts of religious ritual. In this story type, as in others, construction of the supernatural supports the theme of retribution from beyond for a life badly lived.

The cast of supernatural powers increases to include the Devil, witches, wizards, souls, apparitions of animals, animated corpses, monsters and gnomes. These supernatural powers are not perceived according to a rigid visual, audible, tangible pattern but may be manifest suddenly in two sensory areas. Even though perception of the supernatural may well be limited to a single character, there now occurs the tendency for more than one individual to witness supernatural phenomena simultaneously. Supernatural beings readily participate in the narrative which may be constructed from their point of view. Of course, most significant is the emergence of the independent narrator who from time to time emerges as an eyewitness to supernatural phenomena.

In Gogol''s world things are not always what they seem to be. Likewise, supernatural occurrences are often prefigured by hints at rational psychological motivation which would suggest that victims are dreaming or hallucinating because of heavy imbibing. In reality, there is no clear link between suggested psychological motivations and the actual moment of manifestation of supernatural powers. The presence of an eyewitness narrator, simultaneous perception of the supernatural by many individuals at once, and the presence of supernatural beings who intrude actively into the narrative indicate a predominant but veiled

authorial assertion of belief in the existence of extrasensory phenomena. This philosophical position was not to please other
Russian writers of supernatural tales. V.F. Odoevskiy, for example, once wrote in reference to a certain writer whom he does
not name:

> He is attempting to assert that all of these
> frightening things are essentially true, and
> that we can never explain them without re-
> lying upon the miraculous. What is one to
> do with him?[65]

Odoevskiy could only have been referring to his friend, N.V.
Gogol'.

FOOTNOTES

[1]"A Terrible Revenge" forms the third tale of part II of Evenings on a Farm Near Dikanka. Gogol' worked on the composition of the cycle of tales between 1829-1832. Utilized for this study was the previously cited N.V. Gogol' - Sobranie khudozhestvennykh proizvedeniy, I, 204-257.

[2]Ibid., p. 204.

[3]Ibid.

[4]Ibid.

[5]Ibid., p. 205.

6Ibid., p. 206.

[7]Ibid., p. 210.

[8]Ibid., p. 209-210.

[9]Ibid., p. 222-223.

[10]Ibid., p. 223.

[11]Ibid., p. 224.

[12]Ibid., p. 240-241.

[13]Ibid., p. 241.

[14]Ibid., p. 244.

[15]Ibid., p. 248.

[16]Ibid., p. 248-249.

[17]Ibid., p. 249.

[18]Ibid., p. 250.

[19] Ibid., p. 251.

[20] Ibid., p. 251-252.

[21] "The Night Before Christmas" forms the second tale of Part II of Evenings on a Farm Near Dikanka. Utilized in this study was the text located in N.V. Gogol' - Sobranie khudozhestvennykh proizvedeniy, I, 143-203.

[22] Ibid., p. 145.

[23] Ibid., p. 148.

[24] Ibid., p. 187.

[25] Ibid., p. 188.

[26] Ibid.

[27] Ibid.

[28] Ibid., p. 188-189.

[29] Ibid., p. 196.

[30] Ibid., p. 200.

[31] "Viy" forms the first tale of part II of the Mirgorod cycle. The text utilized for this study is located in the above cited Sobranie khudozhestvennykh proizvedeniy, II, 211-263. Composition of the tale occurred between 1833-1835.

[32] Of special interest on this topic are the following articles: N.F. Sumtsov, "Paralleli k povesti N.V. Gogolya 'Viy'," Kievskaya starina (kn. III, 1892), 472-479; V. Miloradovich, K voprosu ob istochnikakh 'Viya'," Kievskaya starina (kn. IX, 1896), 46-48; V.I. Shenrok, "Proiskhozhdenie povesti 'Viy' i otnoshenie eyo k narodnym malorosiyskim skazkam," Materialy dlya biografii Gogolya, II, (Moscow, 1893); and V.I. Petrov, from the commentaries on 'Viy' in N.V. Gogol', Polnoe sobranie sochineniy, II (Moscow, 1937), 732-748.

[33]V.I. Abaev, "Obraz Viya v povesti N.V. Gogolya," Russkiy fol'klor: Materialy i issledovaniya, III (Moscow, Leningrad, 1958), 303-307.

[34]T.A. Gramzina, "Istoricheskie i sotsial'nye korni fantastiki rannego Gogolya," Materialy XXIII nauchnoy konferentsii (Volgograd Pedagogical Institute), (Volgograd, 1969), 248-251.

[35]Yu. V. Mann, "Evolyutsiya gogolevskoy fantastiki," K istorii russkogo romantizma (Moscow, 1973), 226.

[36]F.C. Driessen, Gogol as a Short-Story Writer, (The Hague, 1965), 133-165.

[37]Viy, op. cit., p. 218.

[38]Ibid., p. 221.

[39]Ibid.

[40]Ibid., p. 222.

[41]Ibid.

[42]Ibid.

[43]Ibid.

[44]Ibid., p. 223.

[45]Ibid., p. 224.

[46]Ibid.

[47]Ibid., p. 224-225.

[48]Ibid., p. 249.

[49]Ibid.

[50]Ibid., p. 250.

[51] Ibid.

[52] Ibid., p. 252.

[53] Ibid., p. 253.

[54] Ibid.

[55] Ibid.

[56] Ibid.

[57] Ibid.

[58] Ibid., p. 260.

[59] Ibid.

[60] Ibid., p. 260-261.

[61] Ibid., p. 261.

[62] Ibid.

[63] Ibid., p. 262.

[64] Ibid.

[65] V.V. Odoevskiy, Sochineniya, chast' III (Saint Petersburg, 1844), 308-309.

CHAPTER SIX

CONCLUSIONS

Our study has shown that according to the construction of supernatural elements Russian tales of the otherworldly may be divided into four categories. These story types reveal the author's basic underlying philosophical orientation toward the supernatural as indicated through various motivations suggested for alleged transnormal encounters. This problem of motivation may be solved, for instance, by framing supernatural occurrences as dreams experienced by a character in a heightened mental state, which is induced by emotional factors or intoxication. The supernatural being is commonly the animated corpse of a male whose grotesque appearance is perceived by the victim according to a rather rigid visual, auditory, and tactile sequence.

The narrative focuses upon the character who is experiencing the hallucinatory dream and expresses his point of view. Onset of the dream sequence is masked from the reader through elimination of the moment of the victim's lapse into unconsciousness. The dream then continues the normal forward movement of the narrative. This linear movement is finally obliterated In retrospect when it is revealed that the hero was only dreaming. During the delineation of the dream sequence itself an eyewitness narrator is almost always absent. The appearance of a supernatural being is linked with a moral message, the assertion of the necessity for moral conduct in human affairs. In this connection alleged supernatural occurrences are motivated psychologically by the guilt of an individual who has not lived as he should.

A second type of fantastic tale employs supernatural elements which are framed as internarrative anecdotes. Within this category all supernatural phenomena are accounted for rationally as jokes, ruses, or cases of mistaken identity. In instances where direct explanations for events are absent, rational motivation may be inferred from carefully placed hints and clues woven into the fabric of the narrative. In addition, narrators of supernatural encounters remain spatially or temporally estranged from the event which they describe and are usually not the victims who originally experienced a brush with the otherworldly.

The range of supernatural powers within this category broadens somewhat and includes the animated corpses of males, ghosts of women, animated inanimate objects, and devilish powers. The hero's rigid visual-auditory-tangible sequence of perceiving the supernatural being is weakened, and auditory, tangible or even olfactory perception may precede the visual. The subject experiencing an extrasensory encounter is depicted as possessed by a frenetic emotional state brought about by

drunkenness, passion, or grief. Transnormal events are constructed from the point of view of the victim, and an eyewitness
narrator is absent. The problem of mystery is treated through
extensive environmental coloration and narrative interruption
which serves to remove explanations for events from the delineation of the occurrences themselves. In addition, a suspended
narrative focuses upon storytellers who are subjected to ridicule
for their superstitious belief in the otherworldly.

Construction of supernatural elements conforms to the expression of authorial didactic outlined in digressions, asides,
and in an ironic narrative tone which asserts the necessity for
expressions of morality in personal and societal relationships
and contends that the supernatural does not in fact exist. In
support of this assertion of nonbelief, the tales present uneducated, superstitious, or puerile narrators who naively espouse belief in the preternatural.

Common to the third and fourth categories of supernatural
tales are transnormal events which occur directly within the narrative and are not framed as dreams or anecdotes. The third
category we term the "veiled" supernatural because of the absence of definite rationalization for occurrences of the otherworldly. It is here that the problem of motivation is most
acute and receives dual treatment. Encounters with the supernatural receive possible realistic motivation through careful delineation of the psychological state of the victim who may be
hallucinating or dreaming. However, there also exists the possibility of concurrent supernatural motivation manifest in links
between various characters and supernatural powers, mysterious
unsolved events, ironic coincidences, and references to cabalistic
numbers. Such supernatural motivation is veiled or concealed,
and the tales remain purposefully ambiguous in nature.

Within this category the supernatural being is most commonly a female ghost or animated corpse. The victim may now hear
the shuffling shade before he catches sight of it, and there is
a tendency toward the complete absence of tactile contact between ghost and victim, an element of estrangement which intensifies the overall ambiguity of events. As is the case in the
first two story types, the narrative employs verbs of perception
which indicate only the point of view of the subject experiencing
a transnormal state. Within this category, however, there occurs an important initial step toward eventual objectification of
supernatural phenomena--an otherworldly visitation experienced
simultaneously by two individuals. Nevertheless, even here an
eyewitness narrator is absent during actual manifestation of the
supernatural. The problem of mystery is treated by supernatural shading of the environment and the presentation of allegedly
supernatural phenomena which are never motivated one way or

148

the other. The narrator neither asserts nor denies any particular motivation for events, and the result is a fusion of two narrative modes which render the tales subject to dual interpretation.

The fourth story type presents demonic powers which enter directly into the narrative. The Devil himself in undisguised form now enters the cast of characters which populate these tales, as do wizards, gnomes, monsters, and even animal apparitions. The supernatural once more occurs in connection with the assertion of a moral, here an indication of eventual retribution for the evil which one may sow in the world.

Within this category there occur the final steps leading to complete objectification of supernatural phenomena. Supernatural powers appear simultaneously to many individuals, and the narrative may be constructed so as to reflect their point of view. Final objectification is achieved through the presence of an eyewitness narrator who emerges to corroborate a supernatural visitation from his own viewpoint or who may provide clarification at climactic points within the narrative by describing events incomprehensible even to the victim himself.

Perception of supernatural powers may be visual, audial, or tactile and may appear in two areas simultaneously, an effect which enhances the total horrific picture of events. The problem of mystery is treated through supernatural shading of the environment and the disclosure of possible psychological factors which might indicate that the victim is merely hallucinating or dreaming. However, these possible motivating factors usually bear no direct link with the manifestation of supernatural phenomena, and definite rational motivation for events is not present. On the other hand, the presence of an eyewitness narrator who verifies that a transnormal act is indeed occurring and simultaneous perception of otherworldy beings by many individuals indicate supernatural motivation for events and support an underlying authorial predisposition toward belief in the existence of the supernatural.

Construction of the supernatural elements within these tales seems to be subject to certain compositional laws. The supernatural encounter itself follows the same basic pattern of development within each category. The future victim of an otherworldly visit is presented in a rather demented state of mind which is motivated by guilt, liquor, passion, or fear. Occurrences of the supernatural are either preceded or immediately followed by the victim's lapse into unconsciousness or sleep. Even though these tales are replete with threatening shades, hissing corpses, and all manner of devils, it is interesting to note that positive supernatural forces are never openly manifest. At times, however, their influence is marked in the reactions of evil powers which seem to be subdued through acts of Christian ritual.

The Russian tale never presents the supernatural purely for its own sake, since occurrences of the otherworldly are always found in connection with the assertion of some moral principle which obtrudes into the narrative in varying degrees. This educative function is usually expressed in the form of a reminder from beyond the grave that we are all eventually responsible for our actions not only in interpersonal relationships but within society as well. In this way Russian supernatural tales were to foreshadow the subsequent obsession with moral problems and human psychology which was to emerge and receive the major attention of the great Russian realistic writers who were to follow. A glance into the drawing rooms, inns, and primitive villages where these yarns are spun not only discloses something purely Russian but also reveals the very nature of man, for these stories are the result of a fundamental curiosity and preoccupation with the unknown, inexhaustible themes which each age renews and clothes in its own images.

BIBLIOGRAPHY

Primary Sources

Bestuzhev-Marlinskiy   A.A.   Izbrannye povesti.   Leningrad, 1937.

_____.   Sochineniya v dvukh tomakh.   Moscow, 1958.

Bonafon,   K.   "Uzhasnaya   noch'   v   pustyne,"   Biblioteka dlya chteniya, 10, 1823, 49-65.

Gogol',   N.V.   Polnoe sobranie sochineniy.   14   vols.   Moscow, 1937-1952.

_____.   Sobranie khudozhestvennykh proizvedeniy v pyati tomakh.   Moscow, 1960.

Marlinskiy,   A.   Vtoroe polnoe sobranie sochineniy.   4 vols.   St. Petersburg, 1847.

Meylakh,   B.S.,   ed.   Russkie povesti XIX veka.   2 vols.   Moscow, 1952.

"'Oboroten',   ili   starukha-krasavitsa,   narodnaya   russkaya skazka, "   Novosti literaturi, 13, 1825, 1-14.

Odoevskiy,   V.F.   Devyat' povestey.   New York, 1954.

_____.   Povesti i rasskazy.   Moscow, 1959.

_____.   Romanticheskie povesti.   Leningrad, 1929.

_____.   Russkie nochi.   Munich, 1967.

_____.   Sochineniya v tryokh tomakh.   Moscow, 1844.

Petrov,   I.   "Mefistofel'," Teleskop, XXXIII, 1836, 26-50.

Pushkin,   A.S.   Polnoe sobranie sochineniy.   10 vols.   Moscow-Leningrad, 1949.

_____.   Sochineniya v tryokh tomakh.   Moscow, 1954.

_____.   "Uedinnyonyy domik na vasil'evskom ostrove," Biblioteka velikikh pisateley: Pushkin,   VI.   Petrograd,   1915, 19-24.

Somov,   Orest.   Selected Prose in Russian, J. Mersereau, Jr. and George Harjan,   eds.   Michigan Slavic Materials, No. 11, Ann Arbor, 1974.

Vel'tman, A.F. Povesti. Moscow, 1837.

_____. Povesti. M.D. Olkhin, 1843.

Secondary Sources:

Abaev, V.I. "Obraz Viya v povesti N.V. Gogolya," Russkiy fol'klor: materialy i issledovaniya, III. Moscow, 1958, 303-307.

Abramovich, G.L. "K voprosu ob idee povesti-skazki N.V. Gogolya 'Viy'," Problemy teorii i istorii literatury, V.I. Kulesov, R.M. Samarin and A.G. Sokolov, eds. Moscow, 1971.

Al'betkova, R.I. "Fantasticheskie obrazy v russkom romantizme 30-kh godov XIX v.," Iz istorii russkogo romantizma: sbornik statey, N.A. Gulyaev, A.F. Kireeva, A.M. Mikeshin, K.G. Petrosov, and V.M. Potyavin, eds., Kemerovo, 1971.

Almedingen, E.M. "The Supernatural in Russian Literature," Essays by Divers Hands. London, 1960, 68-84.

Annenskiy, I. "Forma fantasticheskogo u Gogolya," Russkaya Shkola (1890) 10, 93-104.

Bagby, L. "The Prose Fiction of Aleksandr Alexsandrovich Bestuzhev-Marlinskiy." Unpublished Doctoral dissertation, University of Michigan, 1972.

Bazanov, V. "Povesti o lyudyakh i strastyakh. Narodnaya fantastika v povestyakh Bestuzheva-Marlinskogo," Ocherki dekabristskoy literatury. Moscow, 1953, 371-388.

Bocharov, S.G. "O smysle 'Grobovshchika'," Kontekst 1973. Literaturno-teoreticheskie issledovaniya. Moscow, 1974, 196-230.

Busch, R.L. "Freneticist Literature in the Russian Romanticist Period: Narrative Prose of the Early 1830's." Unpublished Doctoral dissertation, University of Michigan, 1972.

Bukhstab, B. "Pervye romany Vel'tmana," Russkaya proza, B. Eykhenbaum and Yu. Tynyanov, eds. The Hague, 1963, 192-231.

Chizhevskiy, D. History of Nineteenth-Century Russian Literature, I. Nashville, 1974.

Chkhaidze, L.V. "O real'nom znachenii motiva tryokh kart v 'Pikovoy dame'," Pushkin: issledovaniya i materialy, III. Moscow-Leningrad, 1960, 455-460.

Driessen, F.C. Gogol as a Short Story Writer. The Hague, 1965.

Efimova, Z.S. "Nachal'nyy period literaturnoy deyatel'nosti A.F. Vel'tmana," Russkiy romantizm. Sbornik statey, A.I. Beletskiy, ed. Leningrad, 1927.

Erlich, V. Gogol. New Haven and London, 1969.

Ermilova, L. Ya. "O printsipakh tipizatsii v povestyakh Gogolya 'Vechera po khutore bliz Dikan'ki'," Uchyonye zapiski Moskovskogo gosudarstvennogo pedagogicheskogo instituta. Voprosy russkoy literatury, (1969), 315, 79-93.

Eykhenbaum, B.M. Skvoz' literaturu: sbornik statey. Leningrad, 1924.

Gebhard, J.G. "The Early Novels of A.F. Vel'tman," Unpublished Doctoral dissertation, University of Indiana, 1968.

Gershenzon, "Sny Pushkina," Stat'i o Pushkine. Istoriya i teoriya iskusstv, vyp. 1, Moscow, 1926, 96-110.

Gippius, V. Gogol'. Leningrad, 1924.

Glukhov, A.I. "Fantasticheskie obrazy v russkom romantizme 30-kh godov XIX veka," Iz istorii russkogo romantizma. Sbornik statey, vyp. I. Kemerovo, 1971, 86-101.

Gramzina, T.Z. "Istoricheskie i sotsial'nye korni fantastiki rannego Gogolya," Materialy XXIII nauchnoy konferentsii volgogradskogo pedagogicheskogo instituta. Voprosy russkoy i zarubezhnoy literatury. Volgograd, 1969, 248-251.

_____. "'Vecher nakanune Ivana Kupala' N.V. Gogolya," Uchyonye zapiski volgogradskogo pedagogicheskogo instituta. Voprosy russkoy i zarubezhnoy literatury. Volgograd, 30, 1970, 173-189.

_____. "Vidy fantasticheskogo v tvorchestve Gogolya," Uchyonye zapiski kirgizskogo gosudarstvennogo universiteta, vyp. 5. Frunze.

Gukovskiy, G.A. Pushkin i problemy realisticheskogo stilya. Moscow, 1957.

Gus, M. Gogol' i nikolaevskaya Rossiya. Moscow, 1957.

Il'enkov, E.V. "Ob esteticheskoy prirode fantazii," Sbornik: voprosy estetiki #6. Moscow, 1964.

Ilyinsky, O.P. "Some Fundamental Problems of Russian Romanticism (Based on V.F. Odoevsky's Prose)." Unpublished Doctoral dissertation, New York University, 1970.

Ingham, N.W. "E.T.A. Hoffmann in Russia, 1822-45." Unpublished Doctoral dissertation, Harvard University, 1963.

Yakubovich, D. "Literaturnyy fon 'Pikovoy damy'," Literaturnyy sovremennik. I, 1935, 206-212.

_____. "O Pikovoy dame," Pushkin: 1833 god. Leningrad, 1935, 57-68.

Kagarlitskiy, Yu. "Realizm i fantastika," Voprosy literatury. I, 1971.

Kashin, N.P. "Po povodu 'Pikovoy damy'," Pushkin i ego sovremenniki. XXXI-XXXIII, 1927, 25-34.

Kodjak, A. "'The Queen of Spades' in the Context of the Faust Legend," Alexander Pushkin: A Symposium on the 175th Anniversary of his Birth. New York, 1976, 87-118.

_____. "Ustnaya rech' Pushkina v zapisi Titova," American Contributions to the Seventh International Congress of Slavists. II, 1973, 321-337.

Kotlyarevskiy, N. Dekabristy: Kn. A. Odoevskiy i A. Bestuzhev-Marlinskiy. St. Petersburg, 1907.

_____. Nikolay Vasil'evich Gogol' 1829-1842. St. Petersburg, 1908.

Kramchanin, A.I. "O printsipakh tipizatsii v povestyakh Gogolya 'Vechera na khutore bliz Dikan'ki'," Uchyonye zapiski moskovskogo gosudarstvennogo pedagogicheskogo instituta. 315, 1969, 79-93.

Leighton, L. "Aleksandr Bestuzhev-Marlinskiy: The Romantic Prose Tale in Russia," Unpublished Doctoral dissertation, University of Wisconsin, 1968.

Lerner, N.O. "Istoriya 'Pikovoy damy'," Rasskazy o Pushkine. Leningrad, 1929, 132-163.

Lerner, N.O. Proza Pushkina. Petrograd-Moscow, 1923.

Linburn, J.H. "A Would-Be Faust: Vladimir Fyodorovich Odoevsky and his Prose Fiction, 1830-1845." Unpublished Doctoral dissertation, Columbia University, 1970.

Lotman, Yu. M. "Iz nablyudeniy nad strukturnymi printsipami rannego tvorchestva Gogolya," Uchyonye zapiski tartuskogo universiteta. Trudy po russkoy i slavyanskoy filologii, XV, 251, 1970, 17-45.

_____. Lektsii po struktural'noy poetike. Providence, 1968.

Lovecraft, H.P. Supernatural Horror in Literature. New York, 1945.

Mann, Yu. V. "Evolyutsiya gogolevskoy fantastiki," K istorii russkogo romantizma, Yu. V. Mann, I.G. Neupokoeva and U.R. Fokht, Eds., Moscow, 1973.

Meylakh, B.S. Pushkin i russkiy romantizm. Moscow-Leningrad, 1937.

Miloradovich, V. "K voprosu ob istochnikakh 'Viya'," Kievskaya starina, kn. 9, 1896, 46-48.

Nabokov, V., ed. and tr. Eugene Onegin. New York, 1964.

Nazarevskiy, A.A. "Viy v povesti Gogolya i Kas'yan v narodnykh pover'yakh o 29 fevralya," Voprosy russkoy literatury, 3, 1969, 39-46.

Ovsianiko-Kulikovskiy, D.N. Istoriya russkoy literatury XIX v., vols. 1-2, Moscow, 1910.

Passage, C.E. The Russian Hoffmanists. The Hague, 1963.

Penzoldt, P. The Supernatural in Fiction. New York, 1965.

Pereverzev, V.F. Iz istokov russkogo realisticheskogo romana. Moscow, 1965, 114 ff.

Piksanov, B. "Ukrainskie povesti Gogolya," O klassikakh: sbornik statey. Moscow, 1933, 43-148.

Pisnaya, V. "Fabula 'Uedinnyonogo domika na vasil'evskom'," Pushkin i ego sovremenniki, XXXI-XXXII, 1927, 19-24.

Pospelov, G.N. Tvorchestvo N.V. Gogolya. Moscow, 1953.

Praz, M. The Romantic Agony. London, 1951.

Proskurina, Yu. M. "E.T.A. Gofman i V.F. Odoevskiy: k voprosu o natsional'noy spetsifike fantastiki," Uchyonye zapiski sverdlovskogo pedagogicheskogo instituta i tyumenskogo pedagogicheskogo instituta. 2, sb. 118, 1970, 109-122.

Rosen, N. "The Magic Cards in 'The Queen of Spades'," Slavic and East European Journal, 19, 4, 1975, 255-275.

Sakulin, P.M. Iz istorii russkogo idealizma. Knyaz' V.F. Odoevskiy, myslitel'-pisatel'. Moscow, 1913.

Scott, Sir W. Lives of Eminent Novelists and Dramatists. London, 1887.

_____. "On the Supernatural in Fictitious Composition," Foreign Quarterly Review. July, 1827, 60-98.

Semibratova, I.V. "K istorii voprosa o russkoy fantasticheskoy proze 30-kh godov XIX veka," Vestnik moskovskogo universiteta. 4, 1972, 18-28.

Setchkareff, V. Gogol: His Life and Works. New York, 1965.

Sharoeva, T.G. "Russkaya povest' kontsa 20-kh-nachala 30-kh godov," Doklady AnAzSSR. 2, 1958.

Shaw, J.T. "The 'Conclusion' of Pushkin's 'Queen of Spades'," Studies in Russian and Polish Literature. Zbigniew Folejewski et al., eds. The Hague, 1962, 119 ff.

Shenrok, V.I. "Proiskhozhdenie povesti 'Viy' i otnoshenie eyo k narodnym malorosiyskim skazkam," Materialy dlya biografii Gogolya. II, Moscow, 1893.

Shevyryov, S.P. "'Dvoynik' A. Pogorel'skogo," Moskovskiy vestnik, ch. 10, 14, 1828, 160.

Shteyn, S. Pushkin i Gofman: sravnitel'noe literaturnoe issledovanie. Derpt, 1927.

Shurig-Geick, D. Studien zum modernen "conte fantastique." Heidelberg, 1970.

Sipovskiy, V.V. Istoriya russkoy slovesnosti. ch. 3, vyp. 1, St. Petersburg, 1911.

Slonimskiy, A. "O kompozitsii 'Pikovoy damy'," Pushkinist: pushkinskiy sbornik pamyati S.A. Vengerova, S.V. Yakovleva, ed. IV. 1922, 171-180.

Stender-Peterson, A. "Der ursprung des Gogolschen Teufels," Goteborgs Hogskolas Arsskrift, 1926, 72 ff.

Stepanov, N.L. N.V. Gogol': Tvorcheskiy put'. Moscow, 1959.

_____. "Povest' 30-kh godov," Starinnaya povest'. Leningrad, 1929, 22.

Stilman, L. "Gogol's 'Overcoat' - Thematic Pattern and Origins," The American Slavic and East European Review, 1952, 138 ff.

Sumtsov, N.F. "Paralleli k povesti N.V. Gogolya 'Viy'," Kievskaya starina. IX, 1896, 472-479.

Uspensky, B.A. Poetics of Composition, V. Zavarin, Trans. Berkeley, 1973.

Vengerov, S.Z., ed. "Uedinyonnyy domik na vasil'evskom," Biblioteka velikikh pisateley: Pushkin. 6, 1915, 181-194.

Vinogradov, V.V. Etyudy o stile Gogolya. Leningrad, 1926.

_____. Stil' Pushkina. Moscow, 1941.

Zamotin, I.I. Romanticheskiy idealizm. St. Petersburg, 1907.

_____. Romantizm dvadtsatykh godov XIX stol. v russkoy literature. Varshava, 1903.

INDEX

163